KU-121-192

ACKNOWLEDGMENTS

Dan Ablan—My thanks go out yet again to the fine people at New Riders Publishing and Pearson Education. I was thrilled to get a call from Elise Walter at New Riders asking me to start thinking about a *Killer Tips* book for LightWave. Thank you Elise and Associate Publisher Stephanie Wall for your belief in my abilities and the extra pushing each week to get this book published. I would also like to thank Lisa Thibault for her professionalism and dedication to this book.

Thank you to Scott Kelby for creating such a cool series of books, and thank you for approving our proposal. We hope to make you proud!

To Randy, longtime friend and LightWave enthusiast, thanks for coming on board with this project and making it even better. The book would not be the same without you.

Big thanks, as always, to my friends at NewTek, as well as Jack "Deuce" Bennett and William "Proton" Vaughn, for your hard work and dedication. Your years of experience and great personality help make these even better. Alan Chan, as always, your additional technical edits and comments are always appreciated!

Thank you to all my friends in the LightWave community. I appreciate your support and suggestions and hope this book is everything you've asked for. Thank you to all the NewTek developers, programmers, and staff. After working together for more than 10 years now, I can honestly say you're the most professional, hard-working, and dedicated company I've ever seen. This goes for Chuck Baker who tirelessly puts out fires and has helped keep this book on track.

Finally, thanks to my brilliant wife and adorable daughter. Not only did you put up with me writing this book, as well as *Inside LightWave 8* at the same time, but you also just put up with me. Thanks.

Randy Sharp—There cannot be enough said about the single most inspirational person in my life, my wife Kathleen. Her continued support and love is what enables me to be the person I am. It is rare when you are able to find someone who you are truly glad to be by your side during your journey through this strange thing we call life. I consider myself to be the luckiest man alive. Not only is Kathleen a fantastic wife, but she is a wonderful mother to my children Drew, Austin, and Brooke. I hope my children know how much they enrich my life. They show me, each and every day, just how wonderful the world is with them in it. No matter how hard my day might be, no matter how horrible the traffic might be on Highway 405, when I get home and they give me my hello hugs, everything pales and fades into oblivion.

I want to thank Dan Ablan for his continued support throughout the process of writing this book. I cannot think of anyone whom I would rather work with on this project. Not only has Dan been a wonderful friend but he, unbeknownst to him, is one of the people who I must thank for providing me the help I needed while I was learning LightWave 3D. It was Dan's books that gave me a continued resource to learn and excel.

I wish I could thank every single person in the LightWave community who has helped me over the years; however, I cannot because of space. There are some who I need to mention, though. They are, in no particular order: Matt Keen, Jason Bickerstaff, Jeff Scheetz, Mike Stetson, David "The Nerf" Hopkins, Kyle Toucher, Edwin Emile Smith, Jarrod "J-Rod" Davis, Terry Naas, Roger Borelli, Aaron Vest, John "Big Red" McGinley, Andy Wilkoff, Rory Mcleish, Richard Wardlow, Jay Barton, Richard "Ronin" Morton, Dave "LightWave Dave" Adams, Jack "Digital Deuce" Bennett, Mike Hardison, Doug Drexler, Oliver Hotz, Aram Granger, Ace Miles, Tod Widup, Kevin "Q" Quattro, John Karner, Jose Perez, Andrew Bradbury, Shawn Spencer, Josh Hooker, Steve Graves, and the one person who inspired me to start learning LightWave 3D, Ron Thornton. I would also like to thank Craig Clark for allowing me to experiment with his ground effect model, much of which you see in this book's screen captures.

Thank you to Elise Walter for her support and, most of all, patience in the development of this book. A thank-you to Lisa Thibault for making sure I stayed focused.

ABOUT THE AUTHORS

Photo taken by Miss Amelia Ablan.

Dan Ablan is president of AGA Digital Studios, Inc., a 3D animation and visual effects company in the Chicago area. AGA Digital has produced 3D visuals for broadcast, corporate, and architectural clients since 1994, as well as post-production services in conjunction with Post Meridian, LLC. Dan is the author of the best-selling LightWave 3D books sold internationally from New Riders Publishing: *LightWave Power Guide* (v5.0), *Inside LightWave 3D* (v5.5), *Inside LightWave [6]*, *LightWave 6.5 Effects Magic*, *Inside LightWave 7*, and *Inside LightWave 8*. He also is the author of *[digital] Cinematography & Directing*, and he served as technical editor for *[digital] Lighting & Rendering*. Dan was also a contributor to *After Effects 5.5 Magic*, from New Riders Publishing.

Dan is also the founder of 3D Garage.com, a website dedicated to LightWave 3D learning and LightWave 3D sales. 3D Garage is owned and operated by AGA Digital Studios, Inc. and has trained hundreds of students around the globe with CD-ROM video-based LightWave 3D courseware. 3D Garage.com is owned and operated by AGA Digital Studios, Inc., which is a NewTek authorized LightWave training facility and reseller. Dan Ablan has released an ongoing series of spot training videos through *Class on Demand*, and he's written columns and articles for *LightWave Pro* magazine, *Video Toaster User* magazine, *3D Design* magazine, *3D World* magazine, and *NewTek Pro* magazine. Dan has been teaching LightWave seminars since 1995 to groups across the country, and onsite at LightWave animation houses and television stations such as ABC in New York, CBS in Indianapolis, NBC in Tampa, FOX in Minneapolis, PBS in Chicago, and many others.

In addition to his daily duties with 3D Garage.com and at AGA Digital Studios, Inc., Dan is also editor-in-chief of *Keyframe Magazine* (www.keyframemag.com), a magazine dedicated to animation and digital imaging.

Randy Sharp is a visual effects digital artist specializing in modeling, lighting, and rendering for feature films. Prior to working in the visual effects world, Randy worked in the engineering field for 10 years; this is where he developed his passion for working in the 3D environment. Spending 10 years using 3D CAD for the world's largest semiconductor equipment manufacturer, Applied Materials, enabled Randy to develop strong hard-surface modeling skills. These skills translated to an employment opportunity, and a move to Southern California, for Foundation Imaging to work on *Roughnecks: The Starship Troopers Chronicles, Max Steel,* and *Dan Dare.* After leaving Foundation Imaging, Randy has worked at Digital Domain working on the feature films *Star Trek: Nemesis, Adaptation,* and *The Day After Tomorrow.*

Randy specializes in modeling, lighting, and rendering in 3D using LightWave, as well as other established 3D and rendering applications. While working at Foundation Imaging, Randy was an instructor at the Foundation Institute—a LightWave instructional facility located on the Foundation Imaging property. While there, he was dedicated to enhancing established students', and working artists', skill sets to enable them to gain employment or expand their scope of work with their employer.

Randy is a dedicated father of three and husband to his wonderful wife, Kathleen. He is currently the modeling lead on a new blockbuster feature film set to be released in the near future. He wishes he could spend more time with his family, and less time on Interstate 405.

ABOUT THE TECHNICAL REVIEWERS

These reviewers contributed their considerable hands-on expertise to the entire development process for *LightWave 8 Killer Tips*. As the book was being written, these dedicated professionals reviewed all the material for technical content, organization, and flow. Their feedback was critical to ensuring that *LightWave 8 Killer Tips* fits our readers' need for the highest-quality technical information.

Jack "Deuce" Bennett is a freelance CGI artist, whose background is in physical special effects for motion pictures and television, as well as military visualizations. Deuce has been working in the film industry his entire life, and has such movies as *Robocop*, *Lonesome Dove*, and *Jimmy Neutron: Boy Genius* to his credit, as well as TV shows like *Walker, Texas Ranger*. Deuce has been using computers since he was nine, and he started off writing his own graphics programs. He is a unique combination of physical knowledge and virtual know-how.

Alan Chan was born in Kuala Lumpur, Malaysia in 1968. Raised on a diet of science fiction pulp novels, he started writing at the age of eight. His writing skills and affinity with computers eventually landed him a job as a software reviewer for a local newspaper—a job that he kept while still attending high school.

In 1986, Alan attended college in Oklahoma to pursue what he thought would be a journalism degree. In his second year there, however, his professor put a camera on his shoulders—and everything changed. Alan discovered a penchant for visual storytelling and ended up writing and directing a feature-length TV movie for his senior project.

Graduating in 1990 with a B.A. in mass communications, Alan went on to serve as a television producer/director in Oklahoma City for five years, where he was responsible for special productions, live sports, and regional telecasts.

In 1995, Alan joined Venice, California-based effects house Digital Domain, creating visual effects for James Cameron's *Titanic* as well as for Clio–award-winning Nike and Chevrolet commercials. Three published books on 3D animation further established Alan's name in the visual effects industry.

The success of *Titanic* presented Alan with the opportunity to become a partner and cofounder of Station X Studios, where he served as VFX supervisor on commercials as well as projects such as Tom Clancy's *Netforce*.

In 2001, Alan signed on with Sony Pictures Imageworks, returning to feature film work as a look development lead on the Quidditch sequence for Warner Brother's *Harry Potter and the Sorcerer's Stone*. His most recent work includes tours of duty on Imageworks' Academy Award–winning short *The Chubb Chubbs* as well as Peter Jackson's *Lord of The Rings: The Two Towers*. He recently wrapped VFX work on Michael Bay's *Bad Boys 2* and is currently working on Robert Zemeckis's *Polar Express*.

Alan's body of work includes several screenplays, one of which he is currently developing—a science fiction project titled "Ark." His short film, a spoof of sexploitation films called *12 Hot Women* (http://www.12hotwomen.com), is currently making the rounds at film festivals.

 **William "Proton" Vaughan** is a seasoned LightWave veteran, currently working for the makers of LightWave 3D, NewTek, Inc. in San Antonio, Texas. William is NewTek's LightWave 3D evangelist. Not only does he love working in LightWave and promotes it around the globe for NewTek, but he is also the recipient of several New Media Addy awards. William brings broad-based experience to his position at NewTek, having done 3D work for print, web, multimedia, games, and broadcast. Over the past 10 years, William has established a strong reputation for his award-winning work for clients such as Compaq, New Line Cinema, Halliburton, and many others. He has also worked in the LightWave community as an instructor at North Harris Community College. His other activities in LightWave user education include training companies such as NASA, Fulbright & Jaworski, and KHOU Channel 11, the CBS affiliate in Houston, to use LightWave.

TABLE OF CONTENTS

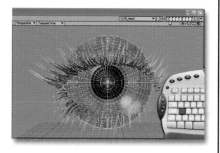

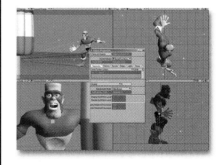

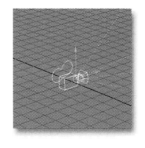

TABLE OF CONTENTS

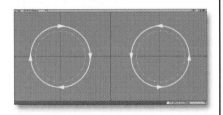

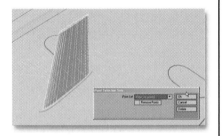

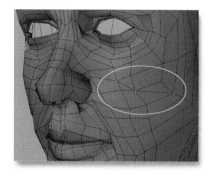

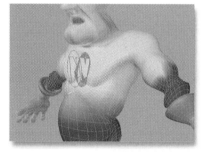

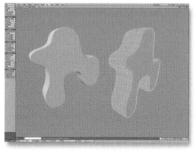

TABLE OF CONTENTS

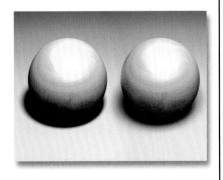

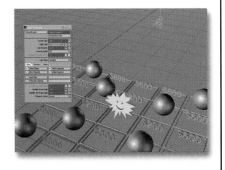

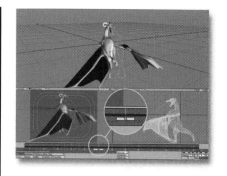

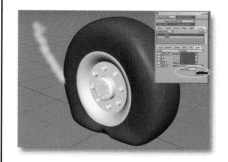

Chapter 7
What Gets Under Your Skin?

TABLE OF CONTENTS

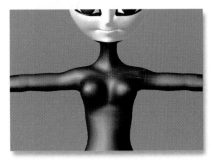

Chapter 8
Beauty Is Only Skin Deep

TABLE OF CONTENTS

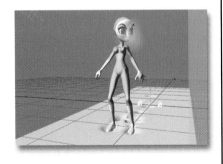

TELL US WHAT YOU THINK

As the reader of this book, you are the most important critic and commentator. We value your opinion and want to know what we're doing right, what we could do better, what areas you'd like to see us publish in, and any other words of wisdom you're willing to pass our way.

As Associate Publisher for New Riders Publishing/Peachpit Press, I welcome your comments. You can fax, email, or write me directly to let me know what you did or didn't like about this book—as well as what we can do to make our books stronger. When you write, please be sure to include this book's title, ISBN, and author, as well as your name and phone or fax number. I will carefully review your comments and share them with the author and editors who worked on the book.

Please note that I cannot help you with technical problems related to the topic of this book, and that due to the high volume of email I receive, I might not be able to reply to every message.

Fax: 317-428-3280

Email: stephanie.wall@peachpit.com

Mail: Stephanie Wall
Associate Publisher
New Riders Publishing/Peachpit Press
800 East 96th Street, 3rd Floor
Indianapolis, IN 46240 USA

Visit Dan Ablan's Web Sites

Dan Ablan keeps regular websites for book information, tutorials, and LightWave learning at www.danablan.com and www.3dgarage.com. For up-to-date information on all of Dan's books, including *Inside LightWave* errata, please check these links.

INTRODUCTION

Elise had just ordered some turkey wraps from a new place that opened near the publisher's office. They delivered, so it was the obvious choice. As we sat around waiting for lunch to arrive, we continued discussing new book ideas for LightWave. The obvious choices popped up, but we needed something new, something fresh, something—killer. Then it hit us! *LightWave Killer Tips*!

After working with New Riders for nearly seven years and working with LightWave 3D for nearly double that, I knew it was time to put all the knowledge in one place. Scott Kelby created the Killer Tips series to fulfill a need in the marketplace. The *Photoshop Killer Tips* book, among others, is a great book. But could it work for 3D? In reviewing the idea further, we realized that this was the ideal format for a 3D application. Why? Well, let us tell you.

You, like many people, work with computers and software. There are many things you know about your tools to help get the job done. But do you ever have the feeling that there's something more? Something you're missing? Perhaps a quicker way to access a panel, or maybe a certain setting that boggles your mind every day? This book will be your handy-dandy desk reference for all those needs and more. It will live with you by your bedside, at lunch, or on the train to work. Okay, maybe that's a bit much. The point is that this book is a collection of tips and techniques that can help you springboard to a better way of working in LightWave. This is done without lengthy tutorials or pages of instruction. The clear, concise, "a-ha" type information will have you turning the pages for more. Add to that full-color images so you know exactly what we're talking about.

Is This a Book for You?

People loosely use the term "tip," but you know better. You understand the difference between a tip and a tutorial. If you don't, please move on; there's nothing to see here. For the rest of you who use LightWave and can't be fooled by slick bait-and-switch sales tactics, this book is for you! If you can run the software, then you can use this book. Honestly, there's no secret here. These killer tips are just down-and-dirty handy little things that will help you work and create with LightWave 3D.

If you're a seasoned veteran of LightWave 3D, you might know much of what's printed on these pages. But then again, you might not. You'll never know unless you read them. Go ahead! Oh, by the way, LightWave 8 is a brand-new release from NewTek, Inc., not just a service pack. And with this release comes a bunch of new features that you probably don't know about, including clever keyboard shortcuts and surprising commands you're probably not aware of. So yeah, this book is for you.

Fine, I Agree. Where Do I Start?

Good. We're glad you see it our way. Following the advice of the *Dreamweaver Killer Tips* book, we're going to ask you to do a little magic trick. No, seriously. Okay. Pick a number from 1 to 200. 58? Great. Turn to page 58, and that's where you can start. What? That wasn't your number? Oh, 32. Okay then. Turn to page 32. You can start there.

Excuse me? Not 32 either? Alright. The point is, with this book, you can start anywhere you like. Each killer tip is independent and needs no further explanation. Although all the tips are categorized into 10 different chapters, you can easily flip through the pages at your leisure and pick up a few tips. You might decide that you're interested in learning a few tricks for lighting. Fine! Be that way! Just flip over to Chapter 5, "And God Said, Let There Be Light—Lighting Tips, That Is." Or, you might decide to just "Keep Moving On" and read Chapter 6's motion tips for movers and shakers. It's totally up to you.

Do I Need a Macintosh or Windows Machine for This Book?

The platform wars…. Ah, don't you just love them? LightWave 3D has always worked identically on both Windows and Mac platforms. For years now, people have argued about which is better, which is faster, and so on. For this book, we don't care, and neither should you. A tip for LightWave is a tip for LightWave, regardless of the system you're using, so don't worry about it. As a matter of fact, there's only one difference between the two platforms, and we'll give you that one tip right now. If you're working on a Mac, any time you are asked to click the "right mouse button," you might have trouble. For some reason, the folks over at Apple Computer left that button off of their computer mice. No worries; simply hold the Apple key on your keyboard, and then click that big bulky one-button mouse. It's all good.

Are There Any More Tips?

Any more tips? Sure. Don't take any wooden nickels. Oh, you mean LightWave tips. Wow, are you demanding! Aren't the tips in this book enough? Well, from time to time, as book writing goes, some tips just fall through the proverbial cracks. And if they do, they tend to fall right onto a website. If you head on over to www.danablan.com, we have a page or two dedicated to this book with more killer tips for you.

LightWave 8 Killer Tips
Edited by Scott Kelby

Welcome to *LightWave 8 Killer Tips*. As Editor for the Killer Tips series, I can't tell you how excited and truly gratified I am to see this concept of creating a book that is cover-to-cover nothing but tips, extend from my original book (*Photoshop Killer Tips*) into *LightWave 8 Killer Tips*.

The idea for this series of books came to me when I was at the bookstore looking through the latest Photoshop books on the shelf. I found myself doing the same thing to every book I picked up: I'd turn the page until I found a paragraph that started with the word "Tip." I'd read the tip, then I'd keep turning until I found another sidebar tip. I soon realized I was hooked on tips, because I knew that if I were writing the book that's where I'd put all my best material. Think about it: If you were writing a book, and you had a really cool tip, an amazing trick, or an inside secret or shortcut, you wouldn't bury it among hundreds of paragraphs of text. No way! You'd make it stand out: You'd put a box around it, maybe put a tint behind it, and if it was really cool (and short and sweet), you'd get everybody's attention by starting with the word "Tip!"

That's what got me thinking. Obviously, I'm not the only one who likes these tips, because almost every software book has them. There's only one problem: There's never enough of them. And I thought, "Wouldn't it be great if there were a book that was nothing but those cool little tips?" (Of course, the book wouldn't actually have sidebars, since what's in the sidebars would be the focus: nothing but cool shortcuts, inside secrets, slick ways to do the things we do everyday, but faster—and more fun—than ever!) That was the book I really wanted, and thanks to the wonderful people at New Riders, that's the book they let me write (along with my co-author and good friend Felix Nelson). It was called *Photoshop Killer Tips*, and it became an instant bestseller because Felix and I were committed to creating something special: A book where every page included yet another tip that would make you nod your head, smile, and think "Ahhh, so that's how they do it."

TIP

If you were writing a book, and you had a really cool tip, an amazing trick, or an inside secret or short-cut, you wouldn't bury it among hundreds of paragraphs of text. You'd make it stand out: You'd put a box around it, maybe put a tint behind it, and if it was really cool (and short and sweet), you'd get everybody's attention by starting with the word "Tip!"

If you've ever wondered how the pros get twice the work done in half the time, it's really no secret: They do everything as efficiently as possible. They don't do anything the hard way. They know every timesaving shortcut, every workaround, every speed tip, and as such they work at full speed all the time. They'll tell you, when it comes to being efficient, and when it comes to staying ahead of the competition: Speed Kills!

Well, what you're holding in your hand is another Killer Tips book: A book packed cover-to-cover with nothing but those cool little sidebar tips (without the sidebars). Dan Ablan and Randy Sharp have captured the spirit and flavor of what a Killer Tips book is all about. I can't wait for you to get into it, so I'll step aside and let them take the wheel, because you're about to get faster, more efficient, and have more fun in LightWave 8 than you ever thought possible.

Have fun and enjoy the ride!

All my best,

Scott Kelby, Series Editor

Demystifying the Buttons

Simple Buttons– Big Power!

Big things come in small  *packages. You've heard that one before? It's true!*

Demystifying the Buttons

Underneath the Secrets of LightWave 8

As you read throughout this chapter, you'll see the power within just a few of the buttons on the interface. The tools and operations available now are stronger than they have ever been thanks to LightWave 8. Understanding the buttons and seeing just what can be done is a critical step to being proficient and knowledgeable about what lurks within LightWave—whether it is Modeler or Layout. Both are powerful beasts waiting for you to tame them.

 GIMBAL LOCK MODELER PREVIEW FIX

It happens to the best of us. You know, you're moving around in Modeler's preview window, usually the top-right quadrant that defaults to a perspective view when, all of a sudden, your object is stuck! This happens from time to time. Your view just sort of spins, and you can't seem to get your object back into a proper perspective. Instead of using the viewport view tools at the top right of each quadrant, just hold down the Alt key and then click and drag directly in the Perspective window. You might find this an easy way to manipulate the viewport without having to go to the icon. Many people do!

 CHOMPIN' AT THE BIT

RAM is good and cheap; furthermore, what you have is never enough! LightWave 8 is great, but like any program, it benefits from having more memory. One of the fastest ways to eat up the available RAM on your system is to load images with color space greater than 8 bit. 24-bit images grow significantly when they're loaded into Modeler or Layout. 32-bit images are even worse. If you want to squeeze as much out of your system as possible, knock the color depth down to 8 bit in your favorite editing software package, such as Adobe Photoshop. If you require an alpha map, it is better to make two 8-bit images than to have one big 32-bit one. Generally, most 3D animators don't consider anything other than 24-bit full-color textures or 32-bit textures that contain an alpha channel. But 8-bit textures take up only 25% of the memory that full 24-bit textures do. Many things you texture in 3D—such as walls, concrete, tiles, and more—do not need to be created with full 24-bit or 32-bit textures. Save memory and system speed by converting certain images to 8 bit by using your favorite imaging program, such as Photoshop. This technique is great for video game textures, too.

  CREEPY CRAWLIES

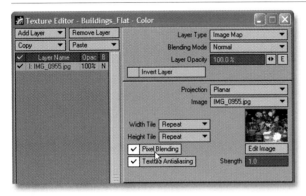

If you have a problem with ants crawling around in your kitchen, call an exterminator. If you have a problem with a texture map that is crawling on an object that is not right in front of the camera, and no level of antialiasing fixes the problem, activate Pixel Blending on the textures. Although Pixel Blending blurs the image slightly, that will not matter if the object is far enough from the camera.

  GOOD-BYE, MR. TEXTURE

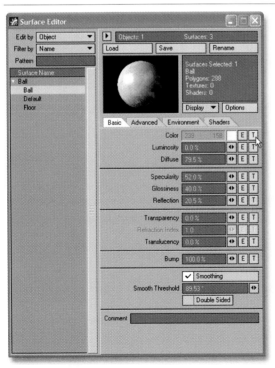

If only removing crayon, pencil, and paint from the walls of your house were this easy! If you need to quickly remove all textures from a surface channel, Shift-click the "T" key. Wham, bam! It's gone! I wish we could bottle that up to clean *my* walls! Just be careful. Doing a Shift-click removes the entire texture reference—even if the textures are multilayered. So think twice, and then click once.

  NONE, NONE MORE BLACK

Sorry for the *Spinal Tap* reference, but sometimes you just have to, you know? So let's say that you have a beautiful shiny 3D ball. You're working your way through your tremendously gorgeous scene and realize you have accomplished the perfect lighting setup. Suddenly, it occurs to you that this perfect lighting setup takes away from the darkness under your beautiful shiny ball. What will you do? Ah, 'tis easy, my friend. Add another light to the scene, such as a distant light. Set the value to a negative number. That's right—set it to a negative value, such as –200%. Also, make the color bright white since it's a negative value; doing so pulls the most light away from the objects. This action creates what is called a *dark light*, which literally does the opposite of added light source: It takes away light. You can do this for anything, not just shiny balls. Add a negative light anytime you want to remove light from a certain area of a scene.

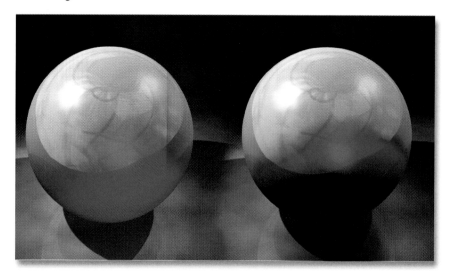

INSTANT TOOL POP-UP

So you're using LightWave, you like it, and regardless of the pressure to adapt to that "other" program a few big studios use, you forge ahead. You like LightWave better, it's easier, and clearly, it's more powerful. But there's one feature that would be cool in LightWave that said "other" program has, which is a quick pop-up menu for all your tools. Guess what? LightWave has this! Go to Layout, hold the Ctrl and Shift keys, and then left- or right-click anywhere. You'll get an instant pop-up of the toolsets. If you like, go to the General Options panel (O), and you can turn off the visible buttons; heck, you can even turn off the viewport title bars or simply use the keyboard shortcut Alt+F2. You end up with a super-clear workplace and instant access to tools with the Ctrl, Shift, click method. You can even customize the pop-ups by editing the configs (Alt+F10).

INSTANT VALUE POP-UP

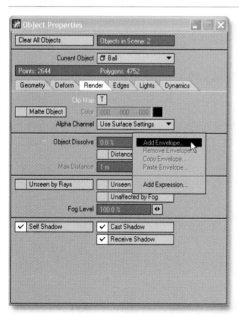

LightWave 8 has a cool feature that can help you work faster. Faster is better, right? That choice is clearly up to you, but we'll give you this tip anyway. Go to any panel in LightWave Layout that has some values to be set, such as in the Object Properties panel. Right-click on the envelope buttons (E), and you can add additional options, such as Add Envelope or Remove Envelope!

   SHADOW MAPS TOO LIMITING? THINK AGAIN!

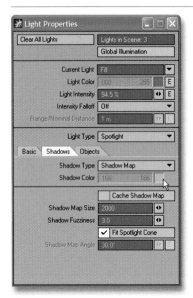

You know that shadow maps are nice fast shadows created only from spotlights. There's no ray-tracing needed! But you might also find that even though you can soften the edges of a shadow map, you can't really change the opacity. Or so you thought! Here's a little tip that can help you maximize your shadow maps in LightWave 8. When you're adding a shadow map, say to a wicked nice shiny ball, change the color of the light's shadow to match its environment. You can change the shadow's color in the Shadows tab located in the Light Properties panel. The end result looks like you've changed the opacity of the shadow.

   VIEWPORTS DEMYSTIFIED

These darn viewports! I can't see anything! You might find yourself screaming this from time to time because viewports tend to get a little confusing, either in Modeler or Layout. A quick tip to remember when working with viewports is that you can set them to look like anything you want. You can set up each viewport identically. If you head to the top of the viewport on the left side, you'll see two drop-down lists. One of those lists lets you set the viewport position, such as a top view, side view, camera view, or other. The next list lets you set the viewport render style—not the render you finish your animation with, but rather how the OpenGL system renders, or draws the view. This is how you see the items in the view: as solid (textured) or wireframe. Be conscious of these views, and you'll have a better time navigating the interfaces.

DOES BVH IMPORT HAVE YOUR PANTIES IN A BUNCH?

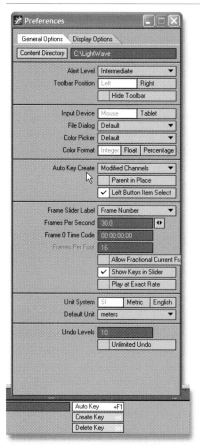

BVH (Biovision format) is the format that Motion Capture systems most commonly use. You can import this format easily into LightWave 8, but if you've ever tried it, you might find all of your characters' bones in one big mess. The movements look like you sent your setup through some sort of transporter and they didn't regenerate properly! You can avoid this by making sure that the Auto Key button is enabled at the bottom of Layout before you import. You also should have Auto Key's Create Key active in the Options panel (O).

WHAT'S WITH THE NAVIGATION?

 Congratulations! You've figured out that there are teeny tiny navigation buttons for your viewports in the upper-right corner of each. You've figured out that one of those icons is for move, one for rotate, and one for zoom, right? But they don't work! You select them and then click in a view without effect. Ah ha! But here's the trick: Click, hold, and drag the mouse! These navigation tools require you to keep them pressed to work. The only one that is "click and forget" is the last one on the right. It looks like a piece of paper with its corner being turned. Click on that icon once, and the viewport maximizes to a single pane. Click it again, and you are returned to the previous setup.

RIGHT-CLICK IS YOUR FRIEND

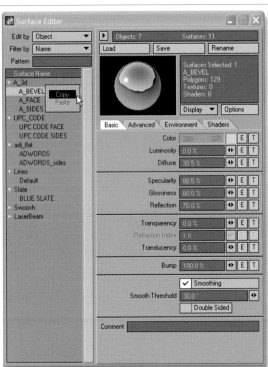

This is the shortest tip in the book probably, but it's a good one nonetheless. When in doubt, right-click. Want to copy a surface? In the Surface Editor, right-click on a surface in the list; then you can select copy or paste. Right-click, and find a new menu to do just that. Can't seem to move the camera up and down when you're looking through it? Right-click and find your way. When in doubt, right-click!

   IS YOUR MEMORY SHOT?

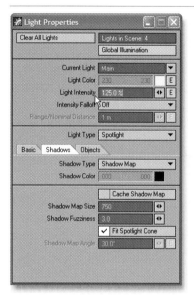

Did you go ahead and clone something and forget to set a value again? When will you learn? Well, don't worry; there's a way around this, and we're not talking about Ginkoba supplements. Say that you cloned a light and forgot to increase the shadow map value. Select the value you want in the Properties panel, press Ctrl+C to copy, go to the new item, and press Ctrl+V to paste the value. This also works for any value in LightWave, such as texture settings.

   ASSIGNING VIEWPORTS TO NUMERIC KEYS

There's a little-known function in Modeler that's really cool. Every once in a while when you're modeling some super-cool object, you need to quickly switch between say, a wireframe view and a solid shaded view. Instead of going through the trouble of using the drop-down selectors atop each viewport, assign different view styles to numeric keys! Change a view style, hold the Ctrl key, and click a numeric key—that is, a number from the right side of your keyboard, not the numbers across the top of the keyboard. A panel pops up allowing you to choose different save options, such as viewport layout, grid visibility, and more. Customize all these numeric keys as you want and have absolute power. Okay, maybe you won't have absolute power, but you'll at least have a quicker way to change view styles.

  WHERE'S THAT DARN PIVOT POINT?

There comes a time in every animator's career that he loses his mind. This tip won't help that, but if you happen to lose sight of your object's pivot point, you can assign a handy plug-in that helps you to always see it. The pivot, as you know, is the main root that an item rotates or moves up. It's also where all things are targeted and parented. Often, this pivot is deep within the middle of a complex object. If it is, select the object, open the Properties panel, and add the Item Shape plug-in from the custom drop-down menu to apply a geometric shape around the pivot. This shape can be solid or wireframe, and it can be any size or color you want. Use this to easily select that pivot when you're animating.

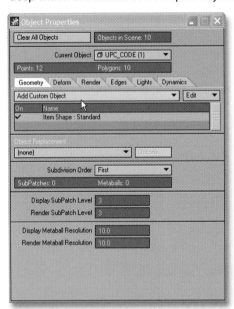

CLICK, CLICK, CLICK, HELP!

Are you tired of constantly having to select the same set of lights over and over? Or how about all those annoying cameras? All you seem to do is click and click more. But there's help for you in LightWave 8's new Scene Editor. Use selection sets to easily select groups of items. Just like you would use a selection set in Modeler to easily select a specific group of points, you can now do the same in Layout.

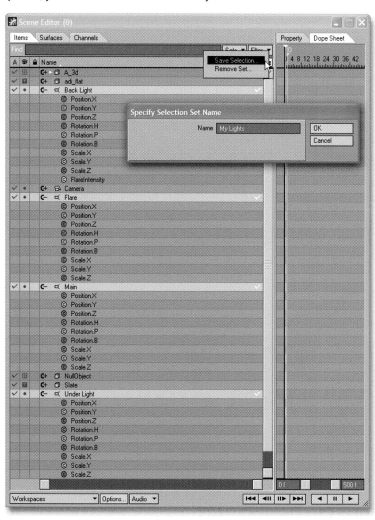

CATCH THOSE WILD PARTICLES

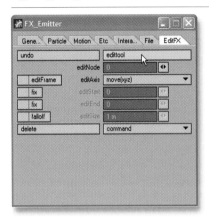

This has probably happened to you: You've set up these great particle emitters that are blowing smoke all over your scene. But then, there's one or two crazy little particles that just sort of do their own thing. Adjustments to the particle parameters only mess up your perfectly flowing smoke. So instead of tweaking and guessing and scratching your head, use the Edit FX controls to remove the unwanted points. Just go to the Properties panel for the particle emitter, click the EditFX tab, turn it on, and then select and delete the particle directly in Layout.

FALLING OFF THE WAGON

Well, you're not really falling off the wagon, but the falloff part is right! Did you know that if you open the Numeric panel in LightWave Modeler, you have falloff control for many of the tools? What this means is that you can vary the effect of say, the Drag tool. What's more, if you apply a weight map to an object or a specific set of polygons, you can use that weight map to drive the falloff. So, you could set a weight map for a character's entire forearm, and then just use the Drag tool to move that arm. It's all about control, baby!

QUICK CUT SAVES TIME

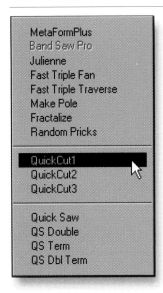

If the Knife tool doesn't seem to do the trick for those hard-to-reach polygons that need some slicing, use the Cut tool that's new in LightWave 8. Realizing that this is a pattern for you, you can use LightWave 8's Quick Cut tools in Modeler. You can find these handy-dandy buttons under the Multiply tab, within the Subdivide heading. Use the Edit Modeler Tools panel located in the Edit drop-down list to configure each of the three Quick Cut tools to your liking. Keep in mind that these tools are close relatives of the Cut tool. Do not confuse them with deleting polygons ("cut" is commonly referred to as deleting). Just select some polygons and cut away!

 ## IS YOUR WEIGHT OUT OF CONTROL?

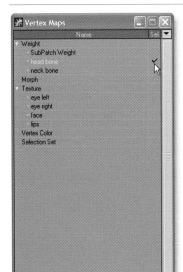

Got a lot of weight? A lot of weight maps, that is? Don't know how to get to them? Does that little drop-down selector in the bottom-right corner of Modeler get you down? Well, my friend, try this: Press Ctrl+F6 to open the Vertex Maps panel. You can leave this panel open and use it to quickly see and select all your weight maps. You can also use it for a few other selections.

Remember the right-click tip earlier? Use it here to save some time!

TURN OFF A TEXTURE LAYER

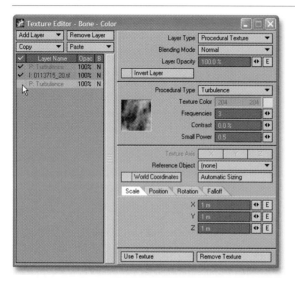

Maybe you've overdone it a bit. Maybe you've added just one too many procedural texture layers. But you know that if you remove a texture layer, or even the texture for that matter, it's gone forever. So instead of creating more work for yourself, which you know would mean less time sleeping or eating, simply turn off that particular texture layer. Go to the Texture Editor where you've applied multiple textures and hold the Ctrl key; then click on the texture layer on the left side of the panel. This turns off the texture layer, but it doesn't remove it from the list. Now, get back to work!

 LOCK YOUR KEYS IN THE CAR

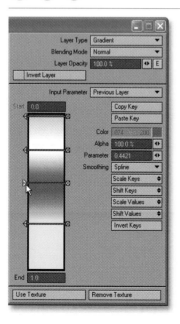

Actually, don't lock your keys in your car; lock them in your gradient. Have you ever applied a gradient value to a surface, only to accidentally click the little X box and remove it? Or how about just accidentally moving it? There's a way you can lock your keys when you create a gradient. Add a few keys by clicking in the gradient vertical strip, and then right-click on the small triangle at the left of the key. This little triangle flips around and is then locked. You can't delete the key without first unlocking it. To unlock it, just right-click again.

HEY SANTA, WHERE'S THE LIST?

If you're working on large scenes, LightWave 8's new Scene Editor can really help keep you organized. At the top of the panel is a tiny button that toggles your scene items from a tree (or hierarchical) view to a list view. List view is useful when many items are parented and you're having trouble finding something.

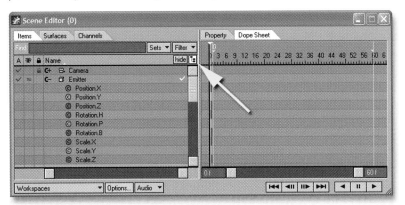

   ## PLUG-IN ADDED, I THINK?

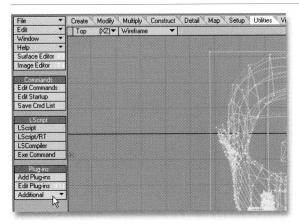

You finally have scraped enough bucks together to get that awesome new third-party plug-in. So what if you no longer get a disc or manual. So what if you had to download it! You got it, and now you want to use it! You've installed the plug-in and gotten the notification from LightWave that the plug-in was added, but now you can't find it anywhere. What's the deal? Well, LightWave likes to put everything in one clever place and leave it up to you to make your own buttons. If you added a Modeler plug-in, go to the Utilities tab, and at the bottom left, select the Additional list. Here, you'll find the missing gem. In Layout, it's the same deal. Make a few buttons to put the new tools where you like with the Edit Menu commands (Alt+F10), and you're all set.

EVERYONE WANTS IT: AN EASY TANK TREAD SETUP

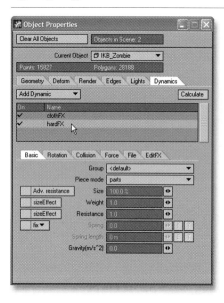

LightWave 8's new SoftFX makes it easy as pie to animate tank treads. Create the tank treads with as many polygons as you need to get the necessary detail for the shot. Create a second model that is a simple cylinder object with the end polygons deleted. Apply SoftFX to the cylinder object in Layout and animate it. After the cylinder has the animation that you need, use Hard Link that's located in the Dynamics tab's Add Displacement list to the higher res tank tread. Parent the high-res object to the low-res object, and the object will take on all of its deformations and motions. It's never been easier!

CHOOSE THE RIGHT PATH, YOUNG LUKE

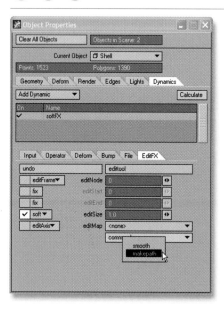

How many *Star Wars* references can you have in one book? We're going to find out. In the meantime, let's say that you have a killer scene set up with dynamics, such as objects blowing up or tires rolling over field mice. After you've made that calculation, you can then use the Edit tool located in the EditFX panel of every new dynamic in LightWave 8 for that particular object to select a specific point and edit a path from it!

   WHERE'S THE RESET BUTTON?

Have you ever worked in Modeler and realized that the Perspective view has gone haywire and you need to reset it? There is no Reset button, per se, but when no geometry is loaded, pressing the "a" key "fits" all views and resets the Perspective view. Now what if you have geometry and want to reset the view? That's easy. Just go to an empty layer in Modeler and press the "a" key. Go back to the layer with your objects, and you're all set, or *reset*, as it were.

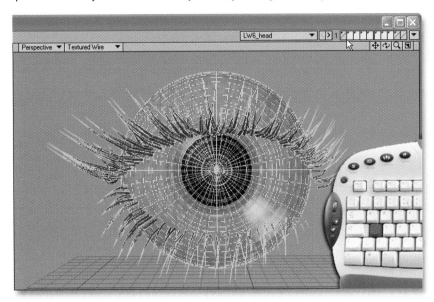

   WHAT ARE ALL THESE LITTLE E'S?

No, not E.T. the Extra Terrestrial, but the little E buttons you see throughout the panels in LightWave. E? What does E really mean? Edit? Encore? Eat? Actually, E means "envelope." Technically, in animation you "envelope" a value; you don't "animate" it. Although certain authors have, eh, suggested to certain developers that a clearer way to label these buttons would be with an "A" for "animate" because that's what you're really doing, the developers feel the "E" will stay. So, anytime you see "E," click it, the Graph Editor will open, and you'll be able to animate individual channels for the selected item. Have fun!

S 001015 1

WTMCS?

WTMCS? What the heck? If you're cruising around Modeler, you might have seen these five little buttons at the bottom right of the interface. W, T, M, C, and S. They don't stand for "What's the matter, crazy, and silly," but rather, Weight, Texture, Morph, Create Vertex Color Map, and Selection Sets. Select the appropriate button, and from the drop-down list to the right of those, you can create a new weight map, texture map for UVs, or endomorph. Additionally, you can create a new color vertex map; or select some point and press the "S," select the drop-down next to it, and choose New to create a new selection set. You'll be using these buttons a lot. For example, you will be using vertex maps a lot more with the new dynamics. So get used to going to this area—it's a time saver!

SI: STOP IT!

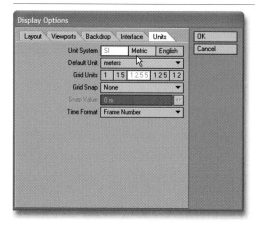

While you're tinkering around in the Display Options in either Layout or Modeler, you might have seen a choice for Unit System: either Metric or English. Okay, you're smart enough to figure that one out, but what is with the SI setting? Stop it? No, not really. SI stands for System International. It's essentially a metric measuring system that LightWave defaults to. The only difference between SI and metric is that SI does not contain centimeters.

GET TO THE BONES QUICK

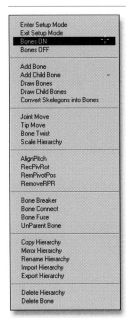

Discovering the new bone tools in LightWave 8 has you all in a tizzy. You love these tools so much that you just can't seem to work your way to the panels to select them fast enough. If you're so impatient, you can just hold the Ctrl and Shift keys at the same time and then middle-click for instant access to the bone tools.

INSTANT METRIC CALCULATOR

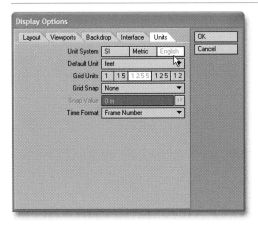

LightWave is an international program that has users all over the globe. Many, of course, are in the United States. Because the school systems teach measurements in English, it's hard to create 3D objects on a metric scale. But don't worry; it's easy to create perfect metric measurements without knowing how to do math in a European setting. Say that you want to build a room that measures 12 feet by 10 feet, with a 9-foot ceiling. What would this be in metric? We have no idea, but we do know that you can go to the Display Options in Modeler, switch the unit system to English, and create a box with these measurements. Then return to the Display Options and switch the unit system back to Metric or SI, and you'll see the converted measurements.

  CAN YOU MEASURE UP?

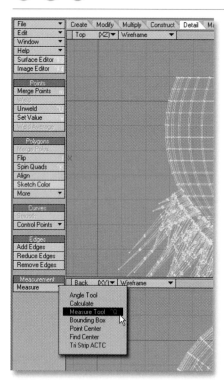

Go to the Detail tab in Modeler. At the bottom left are measuring tools. One of them in the drop-down list is called Measure Tool. Click and drag across your object, and at the same time watch the information area at the bottom left of the interface for your object measurement. You'll see the appropriate measurement based on the unit of measurement you have set for Modeler, such as English or Metric.

MEASUREMENT CHOICES GOT YOU DOWN?

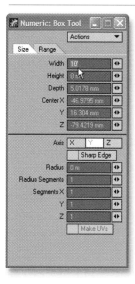

English, Metric, SI… Who can choose? Those crazy programmers just give you too many options! And sometimes changing values is necessary to set up precise measurements, especially for architectural modeling. But let's say that you work with the default SI unit of measurement and need to create a box to represent your office that is 10 feet long by 12 feet wide by 9 feet high. Instead of going to the Modeler Options panel and changing the unit of measurement, entering your settings, and then changing the unit back, you can enter the English settings directly. When you're entering measurement values in the numeric requester, just be sure to add the ' for feet and " for inches. Modeler converts the value for you.

Making It
Your Own

Custom Cruiser

Like a blank page in an
artist's sketchbook,
LightWave's interfaces are
ready for you to customize to suit your needs.

Display Options

Making It Your Own

Customizing the Interfaces

Boy, that was deep. The fact is, it's true! When a new artist sees LightWave for the first time, the reaction is usually the same: "Where are the icons?," "How do you get anything done?," and "Is this it?" are just a few. At first blush, the interface is quite sparse, but that is why, in contrast to other comparable packages, LightWave is able to do more—faster. Rather than having to wade through a number of different panels or windows, almost all options, commands, or tools are a click or two away. Even better, if you choose to change the way LightWave is configured, you are provided with the tools to do so. LightWave truly is a blank page ready for you to work on. Experiment and find your groove.

  DON'T PUSH MY BUTTONS!

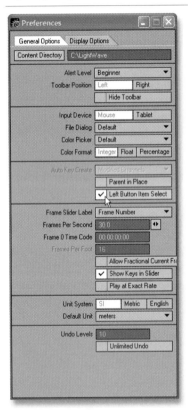

Moving around the LightWave layout can be daunting enough at times, without the added frustration of accidentally clicking and selecting an unwanted item. Damn when that happens! Here's the fix: Go to the Options panel in Layout by pressing the "o" key. (That's o, as in "oh!") In this panel, make sure that Left Button Item Select is OFF. Problem fixed. But how do you do a quick item select in Layout then? All you need is a mouse with a middle wheel button. Any two-button mouse with a scroll wheel will do because that scroll wheel is also a button. And, by default in LightWave, that scroll wheel button allows you to click and select any item in Layout. Working this way is deliberate and functional, so have at it. Make sure that if you have a middle wheel button on your mouse, your operating system is set to use it as a button!

MAN, MY FINGER IS TIRED!

Tired of constantly clicking to select? Remember that tip you just read? You know, the one about the left button item select thing? Well, assuming you ran out and got a mouse with a wheel button thing in the middle, or actually already have one, and if your finger is tired of clicking the mouse over and over to select multiple items, there's another cool thing you can do with the middle mouse button. In Layout, hold down that wheel button and drag around some Layout items, such as lights or objects. You'll see a white outlined selection box appear. Let go when you've covered the items you're interested in, and they'll all be selected. The wheel does not stop there, either! After you have the items selected, you can use the mouse wheel to scroll through the Modify modes (Move, Rotate, Size, and Stretch). The wheel goes round and round! Remember that you can only group-select one item type at a time, such as just lights, or just objects.

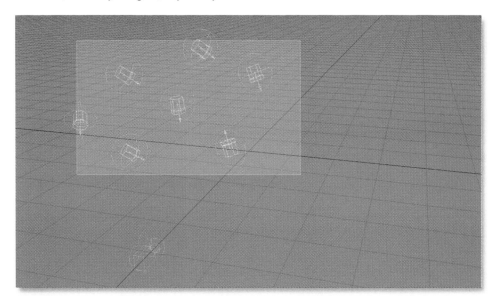

  ## ARE YOU HOT OR NOT?

Is your mousing hand elbow killing you from all the back and forth, up and down movements? Do you operate in the various windows and use the menus? You're itching for something better, aren't you? Hotkeys are your friend! Save yourself some pain! Speed up your workflow! Increase productivity! All you have to do is learn the hotkeys, many of which are displayed directly on menu items. After you have used hotkeys, you'll never go back to that old click-this, click-that method. You also will lessen the amount of mouse movement across the screen. Rather than doing an operation, choosing the correct tab, and selecting the desired tool, just keep your mouse where you need it and use a hotkey. It might seem like a trivial amount of time saved, but over time you will be saving hours' or days' worth! Time is money!

   ## ZOOMING RIGHT ALONG

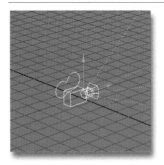

You can actually zoom in five different ways in Modeler. Yes, you got it—five. Having different methods for zooming enables everyone to choose the one they are most comfortable with. The first zooming method involves left-clicking and holding on the magnifying glass icon that is in the upper-right corner of every viewport. Left-click-dragging to the right zooms in. Left-click-dragging to the left zooms out.

If you use hotkeys to speed yourself along, the period key (.) zooms in, and the comma key (,) zooms out. Need to do it fast? Say, twice as fast? Then use the < and > keys to zoom in and out two times faster! If you need to keep a cursor over a certain area of a viewport while you zoom, then these options are for you!

Head over to the View tab, and you'll see the Zoom tool (? key), which brings up a small magnifying glass icon. Click and drag with this tool.

Last is a combination keyboard and mouse zooming tool. Although this way of zooming might seem the most awkward at first, it is the most powerful because it enables you to zoom toward a specified location. To do this, move the cursor over the area you want to zoom to or from, press and hold the Alt and Ctrl keys together, and then click (any of the mouse buttons) and drag using the mouse. As with the other mouse zoom, left-drag zooms in and right-drag zooms out. This method gets our people's zoom award for best zoom tool! You can also use the Ctrl and Alt keys at the same time to zoom in Layout.

"I'LL DO IT MY WAY…"

Now that you know the importance of hotkeys, you need to know that you can define your own. And not just in Layout or Modeler, but both! Everyone works differently. Having the ability to change hotkeys to suit your tastes is another way to make sure you are working as quickly and efficiently as possible. Go to the Edit drop-down on your toolbar and select Edit Keyboard Shortcuts to assign, change, or view the hotkeys. Oh, wait! Just press Alt+F9 to hotkey to that panel! Navigate to and select the command you want to assign to a hotkey on the left side. After selecting the command, choose the hotkey (or keyboard shortcut) on the right side and click the Assign button. Not only is the command now assigned to the hotkey, but if you navigate to the menu that contains the command, the hotkey also will be listed next to it!

Have you ever worked with a different hotkey configuration? Start a new job, and the facility has its own standard setup? Was the software updated, and now you don't know where your favorite hotkey is? (Hopefully it isn't in Hawaii! Unless, of course, you live in Hawaii.) Use the same panel to find them for you. Just select the tool/command in the window on the left side of the panel, click the Find button on the right side, and the panel will highlight it on the right for you!

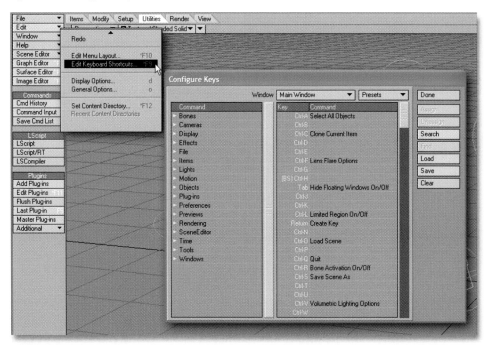

 CONSTRAINT YOURSELF, FOR GOODNESS SAKE!

If you're like most people, you like to have some constraints, or maybe not! You know, those pesky metal bracelets they put on you for driving too fast? Oh, sorry, wrong constraints. Perhaps you're the other type of person who likes to be in control and move a selection precisely while in LightWave Modeler. If so, hold down the Ctrl key to constrain movements. For example, use Ctrl+T to select the drag tool, and then hold down just the Ctrl key and click-drag on a point. That point locks down and moves only where you want it.

Or, perhaps you don't like modeling but still like to be in control? If so, you're in luck. When you're working in Layout, press the "d" key to call up the Display Options panel. In that panel, make sure Show Handles is checked. It's usually on by default. So, back in Layout, you'll see red, green, and blue arrows around the pivot point of your selected item when Move is chosen. There will be rings when Rotate is selected. To constrain movement or rotation of a specific axis, just click directly on the ring or arrow and drag. If you've chosen Move, for example, each color represents an axis. Red is X, green is Y, and blue is Z. This also works for size and stretch. And as a tip to this tip, if you find that you're not getting the movement or rotation you want, don't click on the rotation or movement arrows.

CUSTOM VIEWPORT VARIATIONS

Pressing the "d" key in LightWave Layout calls up the Display Options panel. At the top of the panel, you can change the LightWave Layout to a preset style of a single view (default) or a quad view like Modeler, two on the top and two on the bottom, or whatever you like. But let's say that you select the one left, two right view type. You can put the Camera view in one viewport, the Schematic in another, and perhaps a Perspective view in the third. But then you realize that you need a little more view of the Perspective window. These are pre-set views, right? Yes, but if you move your mouse over the center divider of the views, you'll see that the mouse does not change. Naturally, you think you can't adjust these views because no funny little arrow came up. But did you click and drag? Try it! Click and drag any of the center dividers between views, and you can adjust these views to your liking. You can also press the F4 key to scroll forward through LightWave's various viewport configurations; pressing F3 takes you back.

If you need to pop a viewport to be a single viewport and don't want to move your mouse, press the 0 (zero) key on the keypad and it will do the trick for you. Need to go back to the way it was before? Press the 0 key again!

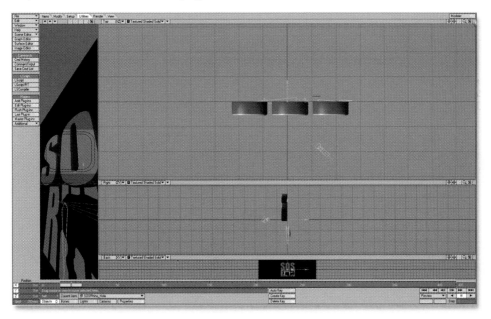

   NOW YOU SEE THEM, NOW YOU DON'T

Having Non-Modal panels in LightWave is great, especially in Layout. However, sometimes it's a huge pain because you can't see what you're working on with so much clutter, especially on lower resolution monitors. But you need the panels open and don't want to close them, which is fine. Sometimes you just need a quick view of the Layout. Instead of minimizing or closing panel after panel, just press the Tab key; you'll instantly hide all panels. Tab again to get the panels back.

   WHAT TO DO ABOUT THOSE PESKY NUMBER KEYS

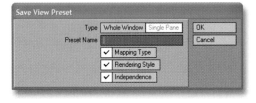

LightWave is cool in the fact that you can easily customize many parameters in both Modeler and Layout. And if you're like most users, you often need to switch among a Wireframe view to a Smooth Shaded to a Sketch view. This happens frequently in Modeler as you work to get close to a model for the necessary details, while also trying to get a glimpse of the entire thing. So hop on into Modeler and set up any viewport the way you like, such as smooth shaded, wireframe shade, or whatever. Make sure your mouse is in that particular view, and then hold the Ctrl key and press, say, the 5 key on the numeric keypad on your keyboard. A Save View Preset panel pops up, allowing you to set a name and save the parameters you like. You can set up different numeric values for wireframe, smooth shaded, and the rest, and access them just by the push of a button. Just remember what viewport style is assigned to which numeric key!

ADD BACKGROUNDS TO PRESETS

The Preset panel found on the left side of the LightWave toolbar, under the Window drop-down, is pretty cool. You can save and load presets for surfaces, volumetrics, or lights. If you open the Surface Editor and then open the Preset window, it's easy to save a surface preset just by double-clicking on the surface preview ball. Of course, you know this already. But often, the background behind this preview ball is black, making darker surfaces hard to see. So, click to the Window drop-down list, and click on Backdrop Options. Set a cool gradient color (or solid color) as the Layout backdrop. Then go back to the Surface Panel and double-click that preview ball again. Now your saved surface preset has a nice gradient color behind it. You can use this method not only to view your surface presets better, but also to help you organize them. Take it a step further by adding an image from the Image Editor, and create a preset with a background texture for added fun.

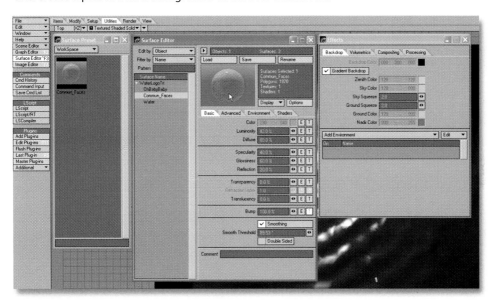

  YOUR OWN PERSONAL MENU

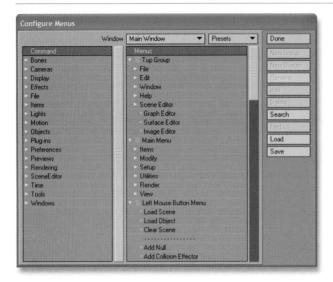

Listen, we all like things customized, from our houses to our cars and even our clothes. But who can afford all that? Here's a tip that you can afford and can change often to fit your needs. In either Layout or Modeler, click the Edit drop-down menu from the top left of the screen. Choose Edit Menu Layout. Here, you can see that the right side of the panel shows all your existing menu configurations. On the left are all your tools. You can take any tool on the left and add it to any menu on the right—and not just one time. Put a tool anywhere you like as many times as you like. You can also add your own custom tabs at the top of the interfaces simply by selecting the Main Menu heading from the right side of the panel and then clicking the New Group button. You can make your own tab of buttons and tools. And if you don't like what you've done, simply click the Presets drop-down and select Default. Also in here, you can save variations based on projects, or perhaps to share with co-workers or friends. The files are small enough that you can easily put them on a floppy disk and take them with you when you travel.

KEEP IT SIMPLE, STUPID!

Buttons, tools, and more buttons. Argh! Who has the time? Sometimes it's nice to have things simplified, isn't it? So try this: From the Edit drop-down tool, select Edit Menu Layout. In the panel that opens, click the File group from the right side of the panel: the Menu list. Click Delete. Then select the Layout group, and click Delete. Continue through the rest of the groupings and delete them all. Click Save and save this as a blank Layout preset. Then click New Group and create a single tab for your tools. From the left side of the panel, select the desired tools you want to work with and add them to your new single tab. You can set dividers and even groups if you like, but all the tools you use most frequently will be located in one place. Remember: You can always get back to your default menu set from the Preset drop-down list within the Edit Menu Layout panel. Save your new layout before you do this, though, because there ain't no goin' back after you choose a preset. Should you delete all the buttons and close the panel by accident, just press Alt+F10 to call it back up. After the panel is open, choose the default preset to go back to your original configuration.

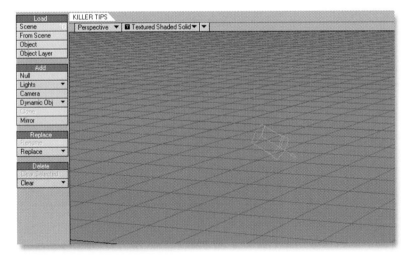

  NARROW PANELS—SAVE SPACE!

Sometimes you're not part of the elite high-resolution monitor club. Sometimes high resolution isn't an option for laptop users. Sometimes you just have to deal with it. Or do you?
Not so! Don't let the man keep you down! So what if you're monitor-deprived! You have
nothing to worry about because LightWave has a tiny button to help you save space. Open
up the Surface Editor in Layout and you'll see the big fat panel. The right side contains all
your surface tools, whereas the left side lists all your objects' surfaces. But in the middle of
the panel at the very top is a little triangle. Click this, and your surface list will jump to a
cute drop-down list instead. This instant collapse option is available in the Surface Editor,
Graph Editor, and Image Editor.

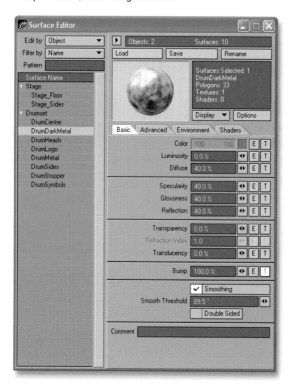 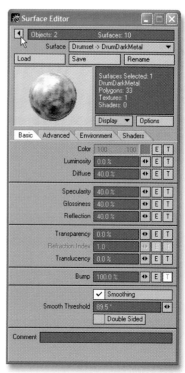

MAXIMUM RENDER STYLES

Did you know that there's a really good way to work when it comes to item visibility in
Layout? At the top of your Layout window, you can set the Maximum Render Style to anything you like, such as Wireframe, Smooth Shaded, or perhaps Texture Shaded. People
often switch this function regularly, which is fine. But a better way to go is to keep this
puppy set to the highest or maximum render style value: as Texture Shaded Solid. What
this means is that all objects in Layout will appear as solid shaded and textured objects. So
what's the tip here? The tip is that you set this sucker to the maximum and then change
each item to be displayed accordingly—for example, some as wireframe or some as textured shaded—in the Scene Editor. This is beneficial for objects that are high in texture
detail but do not need to be visible in Layout. The benefit is that you can view each object
the way you like in Layout but then quickly switch to a wireframe view for easy setup,
directly in Layout.

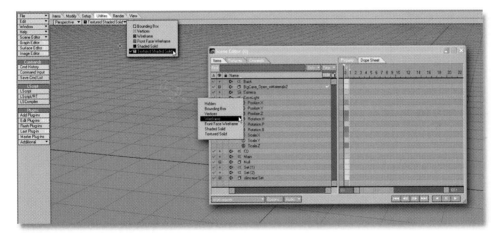

MIX AND MATCH RENDER STYLES

Did you like the last tip? Good. Now here's how you can take it even further. Make sure you have a scene loaded into LightWave Layout. Open a new instance of the Scene Editor from the top left of the interface, from the Scene Editor drop-down (or try pressing the Ctrl key and F1 at the same time). Under the Items tab within the Scene Editor is a small icon in the second column, headed up by a tiny eyeball at the top. This is an individual item visibility. Click on the individual icons for each object, and you can specify for this object to be a wireframe, solid shade, or even hidden from Layout, as well as other styles. Note that this does not affect rendering; rather, it affects the visibility during scene setup. Set the visibility for each item accordingly, such as primary objects as Texture Shaded Solid, and far-away items as Wireframes or Vertices. Setting these details will help system performance for complex and even not-so-complex scenes.

MAKE YOUR CONTENT YOUR OWN

Your content is your own, right? So how in the world can you save out a scene to be used elsewhere or to be backed up? How can you be sure you get all the necessary files, such as images, reflection maps, and objects? Don't waste your time hunting down files by hand; rather, use the Content Manager. Under the File drop-down menu in Layout, open the Content Directory. Select Export Scene, and save your scene to a new location. Oh, and make note of the location where you save it! LightWave creates an Images, Objects, and Scenes folder set, which contains copies of your current scene's files. Now, don't be scared; this does not change your current scene or remove files. It only copies them. It's a great way to back up! When you're reusing this backup, just set LightWave's Content Directory (press "o"—that's "oh!") to the directory where these three folders live.

WIREFRAME COLORS IN LAYOUT

Sure, you can change a 3D object's visibility in Layout from wireframe to a textured object, but did you know that you can adjust the visibility of lights and cameras? Sure! Open the Scene Editor and select a light, for example. Next, click the small colored icon just before the item listing. A color list pops up, and you can set its layout wireframe color visibility. You can do this for cameras as well, and even objects if you choose to make them wireframes. This is a great thing to do with lights, especially if you have large groupings. This coloring also applies to bones; it's significantly helpful to organize the bone structures in characters. This color coding helps you identify objects or bones that should be fixed or animated, and so on. Oh, one more thing: You can also make a custom color. Just choose the custom setting at the bottom of the pop-up panel.

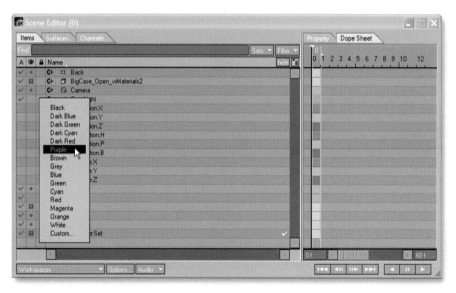

   TO EXPAND OR NOT TO?

At some point in your illustrious animation career, you will parent items. Hierarchies are everywhere, but often you need to see what's parented to what, right? Confused? That's understandable. To simplify, with a scene loaded in Layout that has hierarchies set up, such as a character animation scene with bones, open an instance of the Scene Editor. Under the Items tab at the top left of the Scene Editor, you'll see the objects, lights, and cameras that are loaded into Layout. Toward the middle of the panel is a little icon with some squares in it. Click this, and you can toggle between a list view and a hierarchical view. Quick and easy!

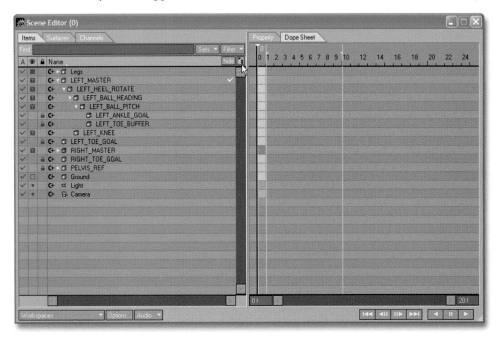

KEEP OBJECTS VISIBLE

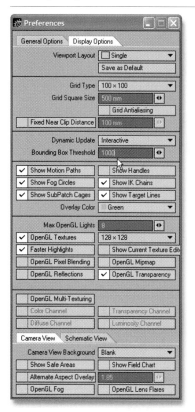

While we're on the subject of visibility, have you ever made a cool model only to have it disappear in Layout when you move it around? What's up with that? Well, it's something called Bounding Box Threshold, and it's designed to keep your system from bogging down when you move items around. Press the "d" key in Layout to open the Display Options panel. Here you can set the Bounding Box Threshold. Perhaps you set it to 20,000. What this means is that any objects made up of less than 20,000 points and polygons (whichever is greater) remain visible when you move, rotate, size, and so on. Any objects composed of more than this value jump to Bounding Box mode when moved or rotated. You can determine the amount you can set—the limit, that is—by trial and error based on the speed of your system and graphics card. Most systems can handle 20,000 up through 500,000.

    SEEING IS BELIEVING

What you see is not always what you get. If you're animating a character and your viewports aren't refreshing fast enough for you, there's a quick fix. Set the Display Subpatch level lower than the Render Subpatch level and your final output will look the same, but your display will be lower res. This saves you the hassle of having to use another object as a stand-in. Note: This only works on Subpatch objects.

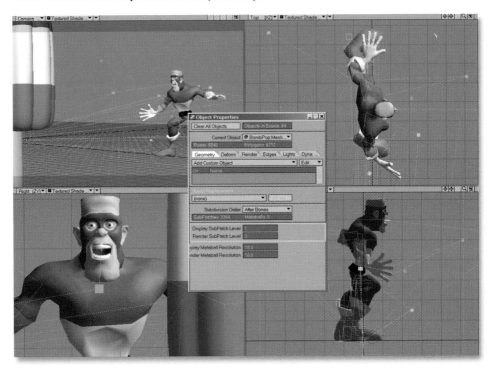

CH-CH-CH-CHANGES...

Change viewports quickly by pointing your mouse over the viewport and pressing Shift+F1, Shift+F2, Shift+F3, Shift+F4. This will be a very handy keyboard shortcut for anyone who likes to work in one large viewport.

NOW WHERE DID I PUT MY CALCULATOR?

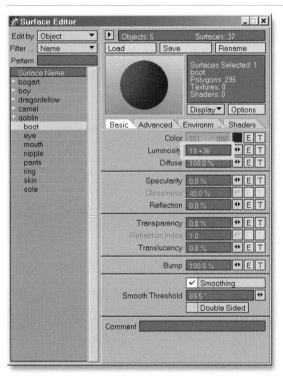

Can't find yours either? No worries. In any field, you can do any calculation to come up with a specific value. Just type the math into the input field and press Enter.

Feed
Your
Ego

CONTROLLED ROAD

LightWave 3D is a one-two punch in the world of 3D imagery. The double punch of Layout and Modeler cannot be beat when you need to model polygons of subdivision surfaces.

Feed Your Ego
Modeler Tips for Control Freaks

We, as users of Modeler, are lucky that the application is much smarter than your average ear-biting boxer. Under its sleek, almost sparse interface lurks one of the industry's most powerful modeling packages. Its toolset is deep, yet all tools are easily accessible, making modeling fast and painless. Each tool is both intuitive and flexible to suit any modeling need that you might encounter. So, put on your gloves, and let's go punch out some powerful modeling tips!

  IS IT COLD IN HERE, OR IS IT JUST ME?

"Freeze!" Hopefully, that is something you'll never hear from law enforcement. However, if you are working with subdivision surfaces, sometimes you want to "freeze" the surfaces. When you freeze a subdivision surface, you convert from its subdivision form to a polygonal representation. If you are using subdivision surfaces for hard surface modeling, say for an airplane fuselage, it is best to freeze the geometry from subdivision to polygons. This speeds up render times because Layout does not need to convert the subdivided surface to polygons on every frame. To freeze, just select the subdivision surface that you want frozen and select Freeze (^D) under the Convert heading on the Construct tab in Modeler. It is always a good idea to save your model before freezing it in case you need to go back and change the subdivision surface.

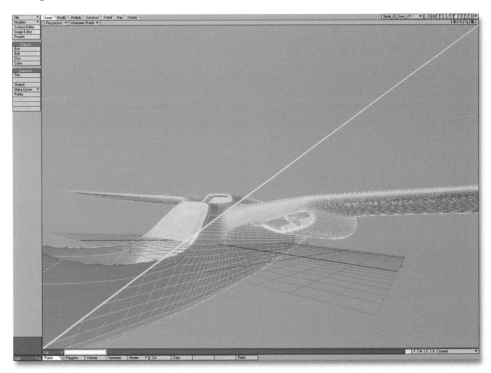

   ## LEVEL HEADED

System performance is something we are always trying to squeeze out of our computers. Even though you just purchased the latest, greatest, fastest workstation—with the best video card—it still won't be fast enough. I know, I am right there with you! If you are modeling an object with subdivision surfaces, the display level (or the Patch Divisions setting on the General Options panel) can really help you work efficiently. Level the Patch Divisions on 2 or 1 for when you need to have nice systems response while doing your work and you have an older system that might not have the latest, greatest video card and CPU. The default value of 3 is good if you have a decent 3D system. When you need to analyze your model more closely, crank the divisions up to 6, 8, or even 10!

   ## MIDDLE MOUSE BUTTON CONSTRAINTS!

If you are a free bird, being constrained is not something that sounds very appealing. Of course, if you are trying to constrain a tool, it is a good thing! The middle mouse button is your friend if that is what you want. Any tool that involves translation or rotational movements can be constrained. If you press the middle mouse button when you click, the tool will be constrained. If the tool is translational, the movement will be limited to one of the 3D axes; if the tool is rotational, it will snap in 45-degree increments!

   SETS, SELECTION SETS, YES!

As you know, selecting by parts and surfaces is a great time saver. New to LightWave 8 is the Point Selection Sets interface button. In the lower-right corner of the interface, you will see a couple of new buttons next to the usual W, T, and M. (That's weight, texture, and morph, respectively.) The one we are interested in is the S button. Select some points, click on the S, and then select New from the menu directly to the right. When the Point Selection Sets window opens, enter a descriptive name and click OK. That's it! To access the selection set, use the Point Statistics window; the bottom of the window lists the name of your sets. Select the one you want and click the + sign; the points are selected! With all the new dynamic tools in LightWave 8, Selection Sets will become your best friend. Actually, because the new dynamics work with all vertex maps, this area of Modeler's interface will become like a second home!

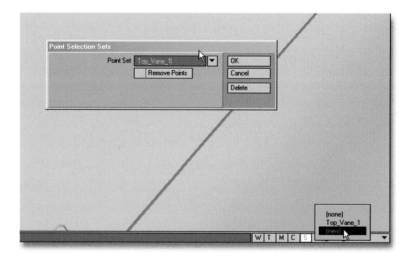

POLYS AS POINTS? YOU'RE NOT MAKING SENSE!

Ever had a group of polygons selected and thought to yourself, "Self, I wish I had the ability to have the points on the selected polygon selected!" The old-fashioned way of doing this involved selection sets and was something that required a few steps. What's that? You want an easier way? Well, step on up and let me show you the new way! With polygons selected, choose Select Points under the More drop-down under the Selection heading on the View tab. Done! Oh, I'm sorry; you say you had points selected and you wanted polygons? Then do the same thing, but choose Select Polygons from the drop-down menu. One step!

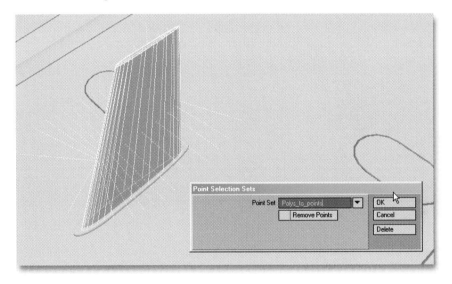

  I'M JUST A NUMBER!

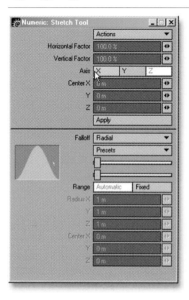

The most frequently used panel in Modeler is, without a doubt, the Numeric panel. This innocent-looking panel gives you unprecedented control over most of your modeling tools. Activating the Numeric panel allows you to enter specific values for your tool or to add constraints, which limit the tool's influence. You want a good example? Sure! If you use the Texture Guide tool and activate the Numeric panel, you will see some of the hidden power—it is only found there! You can also specify Falloff Type and Range, as seen in the Stretch tool. To activate the Numeric panel, select Modeler, Windows, Numeric Options Open/Close from the upper-right corner of the inter- face. Or, you could be smart and just press the "n" key on your keyboard. If you want to be brilliant, you could just leave the panel open all the time—that is, if you are brilliant. The rest of you can just close it.

   KEEP 'EM SELECTED!

Have you ever had a set of polygons selected and you wanted to press the Tab key to con- vert them to a subdivided surface? A quick way to do this is to switch to Point Selection mode and press the Tab key (provided you do not have points selected). You now have your subdivision surface! If you go back to Polygon Selection mode, your polygons will be selected! LightWave keeps your selections active when you switch modes and will have them waiting for you when you return.

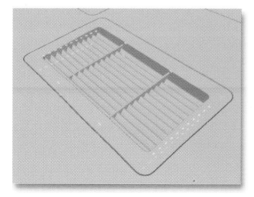 

CHANGE À LA MODE

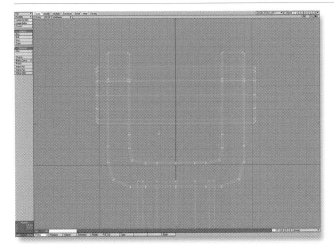

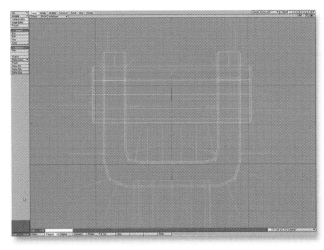

Not to sound like an old man (yes, I had to walk to school uphill, both ways, in the snow, with no shoes…and I liked it!), but it used to be that the fastest way to change from Polygon Selection mode to Point Selection mode was using the specific hotkeys of Ctrl+G (Point Selection) and Ctrl+H (Polygon Selection). You could use the spacebar to do this, but you would have the added "tap-tap" of jumping through the Volume Selection modes before you went from Polygon Selection to Point Selection—not very efficient! Those days are over, my friend! Now you only have to tap the spacebar to jump from points to polys! Tap—you are in Poly mode… Tap—you are in Points mode… Tap—Points… Tap—Polys… You get the idea! Keep in mind that if you have a tool selected when you press the spacebar the first time, the tool is dropped. Was that a gasp of despair I heard out there? Are the volume Include and Exclude gone? No, no. Your pals are still here. Just use Ctrl+J as a toggle to get to Volume mode and to switch between the two.

   HIDE AND GO SEEK

So you just loaded up that 1,000,000 polygon 1966 Ford Mustang that you downloaded from the Internet (it only took 4 hours!), but boy, oh boy is your system really crawling. Screen refresh is killing you! You try to spin the model in the Perspective window, and you might as well go drink a beer while you wait for it. (Okay, perhaps that is not such a bad thing!) There are ways to really speed up the refresh rate. You don't always have to have all the geometry showing at the same time. Why not hide the polygons you are not interested in and get some work done? To do this, select the geometry you want to hide, go to the Display tab, and click Hide Sel. Those selected polygons are now hidden. Now you, or your workstation, need not wait for the screen to be refreshed. To make life easier for you, instead of navigating to the Display tab and clicking the Hide Sel button, you can press the minus key (–). That's much faster! What if you want to keep the polygons you selected? Instead of clicking the Hide Sel button, you can click the Hide Unsel button (=). To unhide the hidden polygons, click the Unhide button below Hide Unsel or, better yet, just press the Backspace key (\).

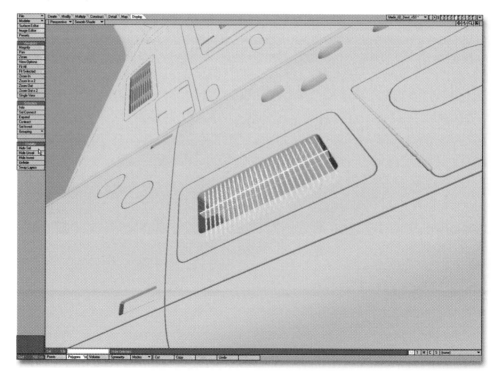

HOW DOES THIS FIT ME?

The fastest way to zoom to a specific area on an object is to select a polygon or group of points and then use Fit Selected, which is located under the Viewports heading on the Display tab. The fastest way to do this is to use the hotkey "A" (Shift+A) after making your selection. If you select only one point, your viewports center the single point without a zoom. If you want to fit everything, use the Fit All command, located under the same heading, or just press "a."

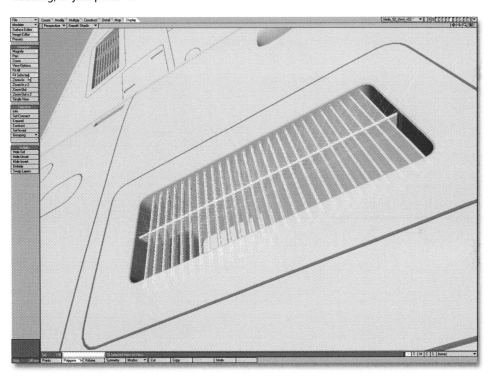

 PARTS IS PARTS

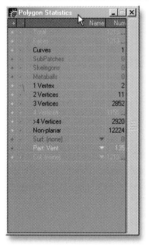

As your objects grow in complexity, keeping them organized can become a pretty tough job if you don't know about using parts. You know how to select polygons based on a surface, but what if you have a group of parts that need to be selected and they have different surface names? All praise parts! Parts are here to save you! Well, okay, perhaps they are here to save you time. The process is simple. First select the polygons that you want to be defined as a part. This might be kind of a pain, but you only have to do it once. After selecting them, go to the Display tab and choose Groupings, Change Part Name. Enter an appropriate name in the Name filed and click OK. To select the part, open the Polygon Statistics panel and click on Part: listing (second from the bottom). Then select the name of the part you want. With that part name chosen, click the plus sign (+) next to the part name. Boom! Your polygons for that part are selected. If you wanted everything but that which you selected, you could have selected everything and gone through the same process but clicked on the minus sign (–) instead of the plus sign. LightWave would have deselected the part. Cool, eh?

 DROPPING TOOLS

Make sure your feet are out of the way; if you drop a tool when you are in a hurry, you could break a toe! There are actually a couple of ways to drop (release) a tool when are you are done with it. You can click on the tool button to drop that tool, but sometimes it is just plain inconvenient to do that. Moving that pointer to someplace—possibly the other side of the interface—and then back to where you were could give you a pain in the wrist (if not someplace else). A really quick way to drop the tool is to press the spacebar. Press that baby, and your tool is dropped; you're ready to rock and roll!

  ## SUB-D SURFACE CAGES—LESS IS MORE

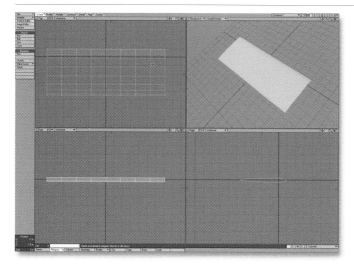

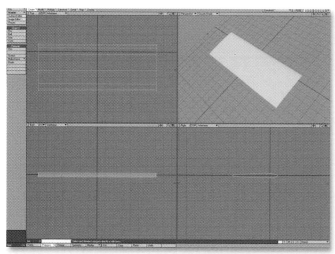

Unlike hot fudge on a huge ice cream sundae, the amount of detail in your subdivision cages should be as light as possible. There is a fine line between having too much detail in a sub-division surface cage and having the correct amount. If you try to add too many of the smaller details to a cage, then you will be left with a bloated and heavy set of points that you have to manipulate to get the desired results. Many times, the cage's polygon count can be reduced and still be able to achieve the control and look you desire.

SUBDIVIDE FOR CENTER FOR MANY OPERATIONS

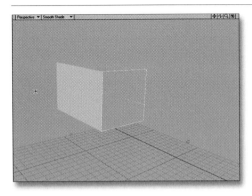

How many times have you wanted to find the center of a rectangular face so that you could get the dimensions of that one little point? I tell you that it can be maddening. It can drive you right up the wall, across the ceiling, and down the other side. But all is not lost! There is actually a pretty simple way to get dimensions. Select the four–point face you want to get the center point for and activate Find Center under the Measurement drop-down located under the Measurement heading on the Detail tab. You now have a point in the center of the face. All you have to do now is select it and call up the Point Info panel (i) to get the coordinates of the center point. Pretty slick, eh?

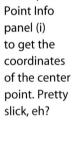

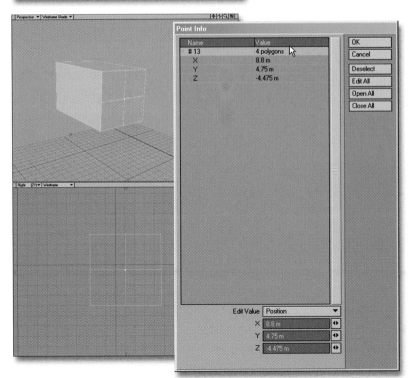

BACKDROP IMAGE AUTOSIZE

So you've decided to embark on a new modeling task. You want to make that killer car you just saw on the road. You did your research on the Internet and were lucky enough to find some nice 3-view (orthographic) drawings! You are psyched! You make sure that the dimensions of the images for the front, side, and top views are correct and you load them into Modeler for use as a set of backdrop images. Sometimes it can be a real pain to get these images to behave properly and get lined up—so you thought. It is actually easy. Using the Box tool, make a box that represents the volume of what you are modeling. For example, if you were modeling a Corsair (WWII airplane), you would make a box with its dimensions. Depth would equal the length, Width would be the wingspan, and Height would be the height of the aircraft. (That is, from the web page, you find out that the car is 20 ft. long, blah blah ft. wide, and blah blah ft. tall. Make a box with those dimensions.) Then all you have to do is go to the Backdrop tab on the Display Options panel and click the Automatic Size button. Slam! Bam! Your backdrops are perfectly proportioned.

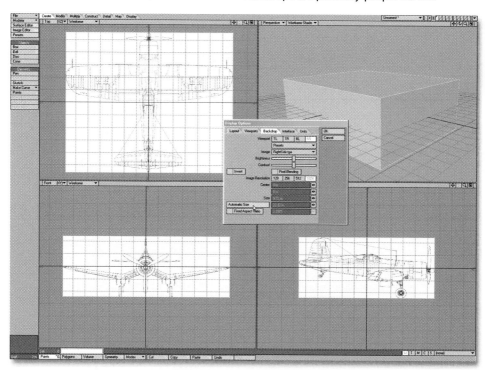

SHARP EDGES TO TIGHTEN SUB-D BOXES

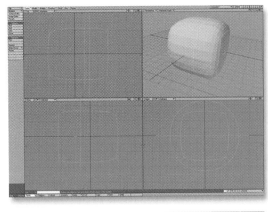

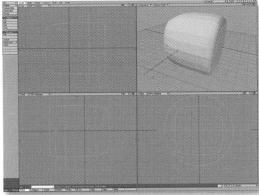

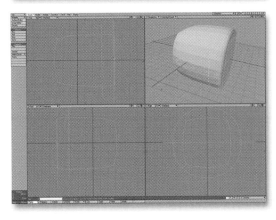

Subdivision surfaces (Sub-Ds) are cool. You get the power of NURBS and the ease of working with polygons. Sub-Ds are slick and fun! They do everything except wash your dishes for you! Well, okay, they don't vacuum your automobile either. Come to think of it, I don't think they even do windows! However, Sub-Ds sure help when it comes to modeling in LightWave. There are times when you want to use Sub-Ds (that's the fancy name for subdivision surfaces. Feel free to use it all the time. It makes you sound really smart!) and you need to have a sharp edge. You could use SubPatch Weight to tighten things up for you; however, many times SubPatch Weight pulls the corners too tightly and makes the edges too soft. To fix that, just add a row of polygons right next to the edge you want tightened up. There are lots of ways to do it, too! You could use the Knife tool, BandSaw, or the Bevel tool. I bet there are other methods you could think of. Experiment! It's good for your health!

BEVELATION

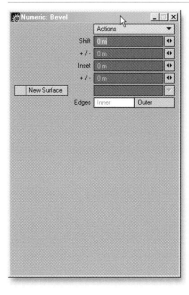

One of the most used and productive tools in the LightWave Modeler tool chest is the Bevel tool. This tool is simple yet effective. It adds detail to mechanical parts and organic subdivision surface models. The Bevel tool is the LightWave equivalent of the "Pocket Fisherman!" To activate the Bevel tool, choose Bevel under the Extend heading on the Multiply tab, or press the "b" key. To get more control over your bevel operations, make sure you use the Numeric panel.

The Bevel tool is invaluable when you're modeling real-world mechanical parts. Most—if not all—of the edges of hard surface models should have a bevel placed on them. Even the smallest bevel adds a lot of realism and takes you that much closer to that ever-elusive photo-real render!

   CENTER ME

Living life dangerously? Living on the edge? No? Then you know it is not always easy to model something when it is at the edge of a viewport. If you want to quickly get your viewports centered, just place your mouse cursor over the area you want to be in the center and press the "g" key. Bam! It's centered.

 ## IT'S VALUABLE

There comes a time in any project when you need to get some points lined up along an axis. Sometimes the alignment needs to be to an existing value; other times you can just eyeball it. There are three ways in Modeler to take points and get them in line.

To precisely align points on a single axis, select the group and use Set Value under the Points heading of the Detail tab; or better yet, use the "v" hotkey. Then enter your value and pick your axis.

The second way to align points is to select the group and call up the Info panel under the Selection heading on the Display tab; or use the hotkey "i." With the Point Info panel open, you can enter a value for X, Y, or Z.

The last and fastest method is to use the Stretch tool under the Stretch heading on the Modify tab. This method is the fastest, but it's also the least accurate. With the points selected, grab the tool, and left-click-drag on an axis. The points "stretch" to where you clicked in the viewport. Make sure to stretch to 0% when doing this operation; otherwise, you will be at the incorrect location. For added axis control, Ctrl-click to constrain the stretch to an axis.

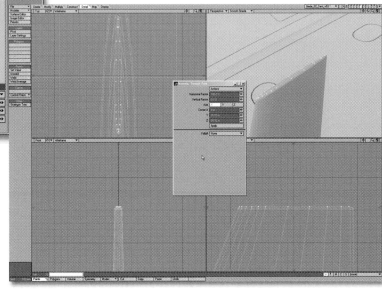

SIT AND SPIN!

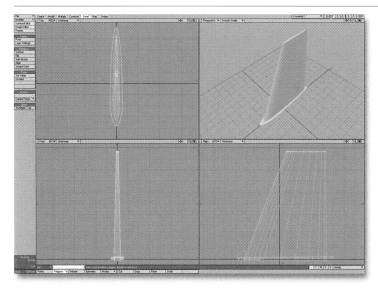

Here is a trick to spin things around faster than a hyperactive kid on a Sit and Spin. If you need a selection or object to rotate by 90 degrees to the right (that's clockwise to you and me), use the "r" key. The center of rotation will be wherever your mouse is located, and the axis of rotation will be defined by which viewport it is in.

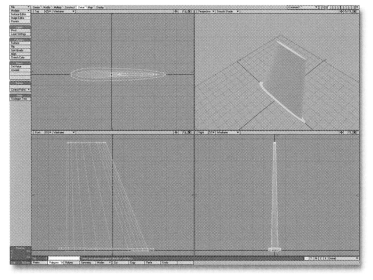

JUST AROUND THE CORNER

Taking a shape and making a nice 45-degree corner out of it can be kind of a pain. There is actually an easy way to accomplish the same thing: the Lathe tool. Yes, one normally thinks of the Lathe tool as something for making a revolved surface, but you can use it to make corners as well. Select the profile of what you want to define the shape, and activate the tool by selecting Lathe under the Extend heading on the Multiply tab. Activate the Numeric panel and change Sides to 1 (one). Then change Start Angle and End Angle to be 90 degrees apart. Ta-da! You have a nice corner! Easy as pie. By the way, whoever said making pie was easy?

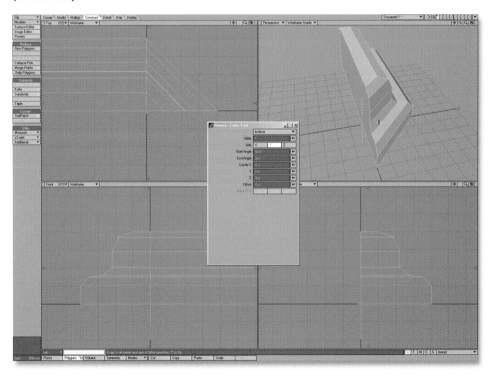

THE EXPANDING AND CONTRACTING UNIVERSE

Sometimes it is not easy to get the selection set that you want just by selecting polygons or points by hand. An easy way to grow or shrink a selection is to use the Expand ("}" key) and Contract ("{" key) selection modifiers under the Selection heading on the Display tab. If you have polys or points selected, using the Expand modifier grows the selection to include the adjacent points or polys next to your original set. The Contract modifier does the opposite. These tools do not work on our universe, though, which is a good thing because I am sure someone would try to contract the universe back to a singularity!

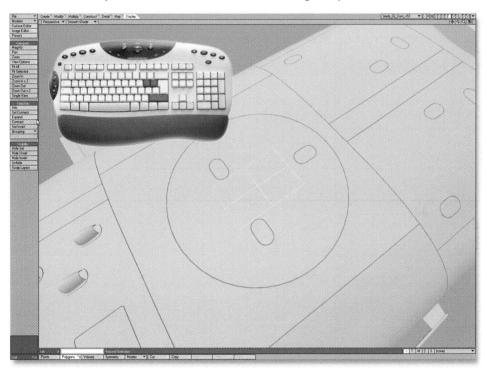

   DROPPING SELECTIONS

Dropping a selection is not nearly as dangerous as dropping a tool. There is less chance of bodily injury. Much like the tool-dropping method of clicking on the menu, nothing gets in your workflow more than having to navigate back and forth, up and down, when you are trying to crunch through a model. So, just like the tool dropping, press the handy-dandy backslash key (/) and be done with it. Wait! There is more! Sure, you can click the interface. You can also smash the backslash key. However, if you really want to be fancy, use the lasso selection method (right mouse button), click-hold, do a quick circular motion around your selection, and release the mouse button. Bam! The selection is gone!

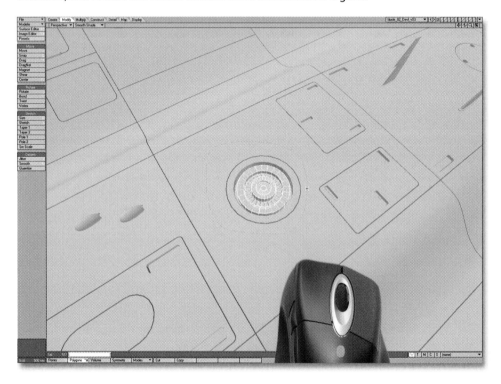

DIRECT ME PLEASE

I used to love to connect the dots when I was a child. It was fun to look at a page full of number dots and try to see the picture before I even began. Then after every number, I looked to see if the picture was any clearer. There are times when you are modeling something that you need to model point-by-point (connect the dots). The process is pretty straightforward. Select, select, select, select, select—Make Polygon tool. (That's the "p" key to you and me!) But the order/direction in which you select the points determine which way the normal of the polygon faces. If you select the points clockwise, then the normal faces you. Select the points counterclockwise, and the normal faces away from you.

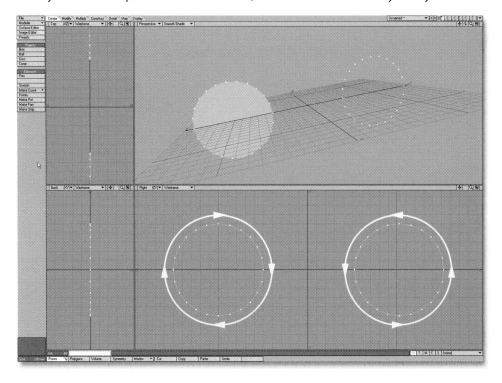

   SMALL PACKAGE—BIG PUNCH

If there is one technique that many people believe adds the most realism to hard surface models, it is the *microbevel*. Oddly enough, the microbevel is one of the smallest details. Usually, microbevels are so small that they are not seen as geometric properties but are seen in the final render as surface highlights. All sharp edges of a model should have a bevel if you want to get closer to a photo-real render. Keep in mind that the purpose of the bevel is not to add a visual geometric detail; the bevel is added so the model catches the light as it is rendered. This single detail gives hard surface models the manufactured look and greatly diminishes the CG look.

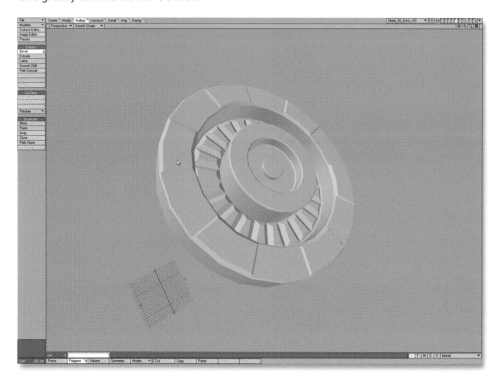

REDUCE ON LOW HEAT

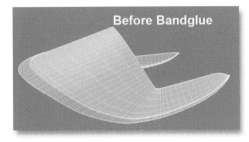

Before Bandglue

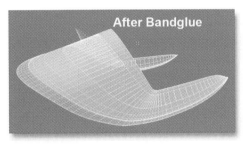

After Bandglue

You just spent a lot of your valuable time making a model for your project. The model is beautiful; every small detail is there, modeled to perfection. The problem is that the model takes a long time to render. You don't mind the long render times when the model is full frame in all its glory. But what about when the model is not that close? You need a version of the model that is not as detailed and has fewer polygons. There are a number of automated tools to do this. However, many times you might want to reduce the amount of polygons yourself. Bandglue is your friend! Select two adjacent polygons and select Bandglue. The two polygons you selected define the starting point of a band, or two rows of polygons, that will be merged into one—thus the name, Bandglue! To make rendering even faster, assign Bandglue to a hotkey. Although many tools are available to reduce models automatically, reducing by hand ensures that you get the polygons where you need them, making your model as efficient as possible.

  MODELER À LA MODE

The way a tool functions in Modeler is affected by what Action Center mode it is in. To change the mode, click on the Modes button on the bottom of the interface. The top four entries are the Action Center modes. Each mode defines how the tools operate. Action Center: Mouse places the center of the tool where you click the mouse. Action Center: Selection places the center of the tool in the mathematical center of the bounding box defined by the selection set. Action Center: Origin places the center at—you got it—the origin. Finally, Action Center: Pivot makes the center of the tool where the object's pivot point is. (If you have not changed it, the pivot point will be the origin.) If you do a lot of modeling and find yourself going to this menu often, it would be a good idea to learn the hotkeys for them. They are listed next to each of the different Action Centers.

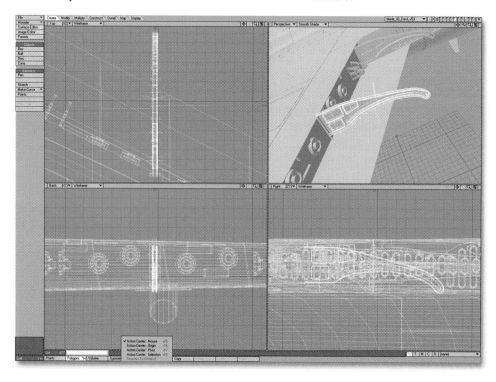

COLOR ME FUNNY

Having a hard time keeping track of different parts of your model? Do all the parts start to get confusing when you see them in the views? To help you see things better, you can set your views to color wireframe by default instead of regular wireframe. Then while you're modeling, select groups of polygons and press "i." In the Polygon Info panel, you can assign a color by clicking on the Color button on the bottom of the panel and choosing a color from the list that drops down. You can also choose Sketch Color under the Polygons heading on the Detail tab. With the addition of the new Textured Wire mode, you will be using Sketch Color a lot! These are great ways to further organize your part assignments.

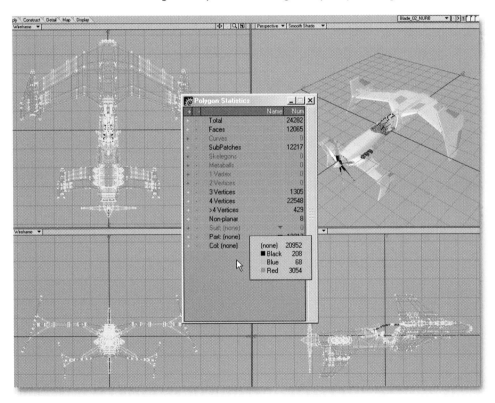

Embrace Your Inner Desire

Construction
Ahead—
Hard Hats
Required!

It's time to cut a little deeper and peel back another layer to see what else you can do in Modeler.

Embrace Your Inner Desire
Modeling Tips for the Rest of Us

The tips in this section are a bit longer than the others, and they also assume you have a little more background and knowledge about the software. Although knowing a bit more about the program is beneficial, it is certainly not a prerequisite. Many of these tips are multistep operations. As you work through them, think of how you can apply them to a current project. Also think about how you might do them differently. These tips are stepping stones upon which you can build your own library of modeling knowledge. Experiment and learn!

  SMOOTH OPERATOR

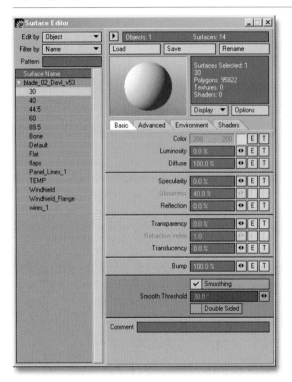

There are a lot of smooth characters in the world. Go to any nightclub, and I'm sure you'll find more than your fair share of them. Fortunately, the smooth character I am talking about is the Smooth Threshold located on the Basic tab of the Surface Editor. The Smooth Threshold is most commonly referred to as the *Smoothing Angle*; it represents the angle at which the surface is smoothed. If you have two polygons at 45 degrees to each other and your Smooth Threshold is set to anything less than 45 degrees, you will see a sharp crease between them. Set the Threshold at 45 degrees or larger, and the surface will appear smooth.

   CUT ME! COPY ME! KILL ME! PASTE ME?

I know it sounds like a really bad line from a movie. But it is actually one of the most useful operations you will ever use in Modeler. Cut (or Ctrl+x) cuts the polygons or points and places them in the buffer. From the buffer, you can paste them back as many times as you like, in the same location, until the buffer is overwritten or you quit Modeler. Paste (Ctrl+v) pastes what was placed in the buffer. Copy (Ctrl+c) copies the selection to the buffer. Kill (K) kills the points or polys. It does not place them in the buffer. The points or polygons are deleted—gone forever!

ROUND AND ROUND WE GO

Adding smaller details to any model can be a pain. It's a necessary evil if you are not into that sort of thing. However, the smaller details are what make most mechanical models sing. One type of small detail is adding rounded corners to such things as a cylinder. Adding rounded corners can add quite a bit of geometry to your model, and for smaller details, that is not desirable. Smaller details are there to add punch to the model, not weigh it down like a boat anchor. So how is one to add something like rounded corners without adding a bunch of geometric weight? One hint: Smoothing Angle.

The lightest (geometrically speaking) way to add rounded corners without adding unneeded geometry is to use LightWave's own Smoothing Angle to smooth over a bevel, giving the illusion of geometry. Here is the trick. Select the face that will be the cap of your object. For simplicity's sake, let's say it is the end of a cylinder. We are going to do three bevel operations. The first bevel adds detail in the Shift direction only. Make the distance equal to the width of what you want your rounded corner to be. The next bevel uses both Shift and Inset. Again, the values should be equal to that in the first bevel operation. The last bevel is an Insert-only bevel. You guessed it: The value should be equal to the previous ones. Set your Smoothing Angle above 45 degrees, and you have a rounded corner!

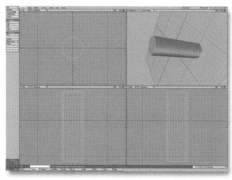 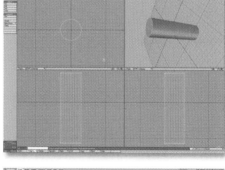

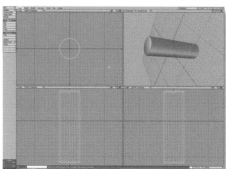 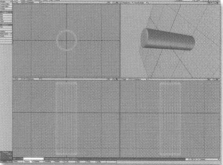

   LIKE IT'S ON RAILS!

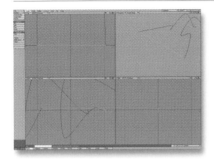

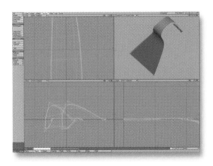

Adding details for a subdivision surface can be rather difficult sometimes. Adding details where there are complex curves is even harder. A way to get around this is to use spline curves with a few two-point polygons. I once had to model a guitar. I needed a way to add details along the guitar body, and it had some complex edges. (It was a Gibson SG; if you are familiar with it, then you understand.) This technique saved the day.

This technique involves laying out two splines that define the edges of your object. Select the first points of each spline, copy them, go to the next empty layer, and paste them. Select the two points and create a two-point polygon by using the Make Polygon tool. (Press "p" on the keyboard.) This is the profile you will be railing to make loft. Add more two-point polygons to create a complex profile for the loft.

Using the Rail Extrude tool under the Extend heading on the Multiply tab, you will extrude out the profile. Keep in mind that you are going to use this for subdivision surface work; less is more. Go easy on the number of segments. Change the option to Uniform and select a number that works best for your application. Feel free to test what works for you. You have the ability to undo and repeat the steps if you feel you do not have enough or you have too much resolution.

Now just clean up the extrusion, and you are done. Because you extruded a set of two-point polygons, Modeler added two sets of polygons. This is because there were no polygon normals to tell Modeler which way to point the normals for the new geometry. To fix this, select the new polygons and use Unify Polygons, which is under the Reduce heading on the Construct tab. This converts selected polys that share the same points into a single polygon. It creates single-sided polygons with regard to the direction of their surface normals. You might need to flip the polygons when you are done to get them to face the correct way.

GETTING THE PERFECT SIZE

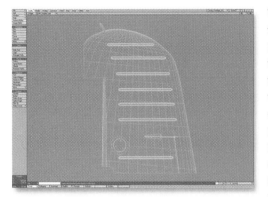

Want to get that texture map to fit perfectly on the geometry when you planar map? Sometimes it can be more painful than putting sheets on a waterbed. But there is a fast and effective way. Find the view that gives you the best planar view of the geometry that you are going to planar map. Hide all the geometry that is not part of the surface. Turn off the backdrop grid in the display options panel (d) so that you are left with just the geometry and its wireframe. Then switch the display type for the viewport to Hidden Line. Open Photoshop or your favorite paint package and then pop back over to Modeler and press the PrtScn button. Switch to Photoshop and open a new document. Paste in the screen capture. Crop the area that contains the geometry (getting rid of most of the interface). Using the Magic Wand tool, select the area that is outside the geometry you want to map, and then reverse the selection. The geometry should be the only thing selected. Copy it, open a new document, and paste it. The document should be the right size by default. You can now paint

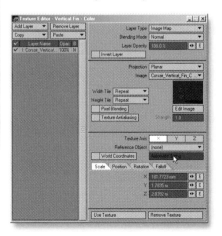

your maps. When you load your maps into LightWave, use the Automatic Sizing button on the Texture Editor to "snap" your mapping exactly to the geometry.

   CUT ME!

When you are using the Knife tool (which you can find under the Subdivide heading on the Construct tab or by pressing "K") to cut some polygons, do not try to stop on the edge between two polygons. If you do that, you might not cut both polys. To solve this, cut through both polygons, past the edge where you want to stop. Then use the Weld (Ctrl+W) tool, located under the Points heading on the Detail tab, to weld the point that was left in the interior of the polygon to the point that was created on the edge. This ensures that both polygons are cleanly attached to one another.

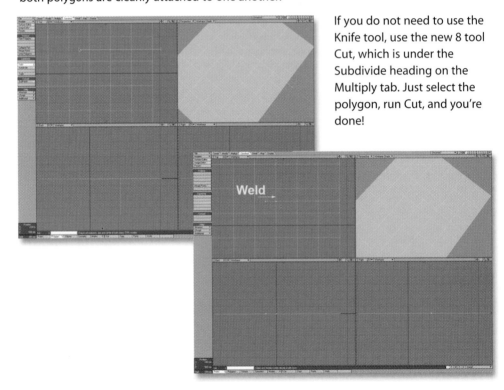

If you do not need to use the Knife tool, use the new 8 tool Cut, which is under the Subdivide heading on the Multiply tab. Just select the polygon, run Cut, and you're done!

  THIS AIN'T NO GENERIC PANELS!

Laying down panels for a spaceship or an airplane using a texture map is great if you do not get too close to the model. But what if you do get close? It might look, well, not so good, even if you spice it up with a bump, diffuse, and spec map. It will still look fake. There is a low-cost alternative, available in three easy payments! Seriously, there is a low polygonal way of doing this. And it looks fantastic!

With your model in a background layer, create an object that will be used as a stencil tool. The stencil doesn't need to be detailed; the overall shape of the object is what is important. Think of it like a cookie cutter. Nine times out of ten, you will just create a profile shape and then extrude it.

Place the model in the foreground layer, and place the stenciling tool in the background. Use the Solid Drill tool under the Combine heading on the Multiply tab. With the Solid Drill panel open, select Stencil, and in the Surface field enter a temporary surface name, such as "TEMP." Click OK to complete the operation. It's good to save out the template object(s) as you use them to build up a library. Why re-create the wheel when you don't need to?

Select the polygons that have the temporary surface name (TEMP), copy them to the buffer (c key), and then undo the stencil operation. Change to a new, empty layer and

paste (p key) the geometry. Add some thickness to the panel using your favorite tool. I prefer VertiBevel, but that is a plug-in you must buy; you can just as easily use Smooth Shift.

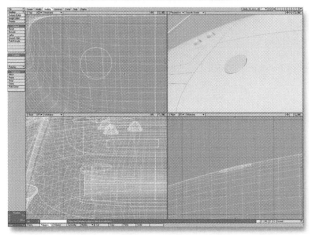

Because your panel has thickness now, add a new surface to it; you don't want it to be called TEMP forever. Then cut (x key) and paste the panel back to the layer that has your model. It conforms to the complex shape and has thickness. For an added punch, use your favorite beveling technique to add a microbevel on the panel before moving it back to the layer with the model.

   BLENDING POLYS WITH SUB-D'S

When you are working with subdivision surfaces on mechanical models, you'll sometimes have an area in which there is a polygon greater than four points. As you know, the polygon won't turn into a subdivision surface when you press the Tab key. You could try to split up the polygon into three- and four-point polys, but most of the time that pulls your surface in strange ways, giving you undesirable results. You have probably figured out that there is a way around this; after all, I would not be writing this tip if there wasn't! To tackle this problem, take the polygon(s) that have more than four points and bevel them with an insert; do this twice. After beveling, switch to SubPatch Weight (lower-right corner of the Modeler interface) and make the SubPatch Weight for the points that define the boundary between the SubPatch faces and the greater than four-point polygons 100%. If you do this while the model is in Subdivision Surface mode, you will see the Sub-D surface tighten up to the polygon. The double bevel with only Insert ensures that the surface on the polygons is tangent.

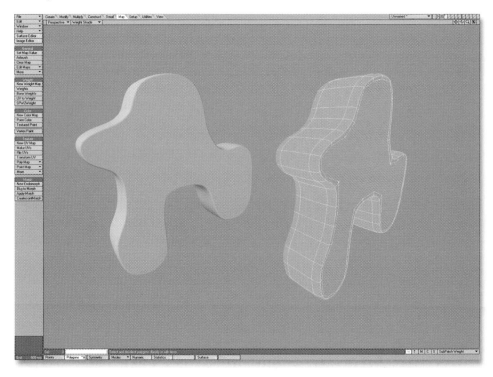

PATCH IT UP

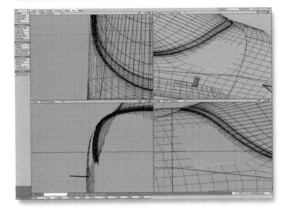

You won't need spackle when you have to patch up part of your model. You'll need splines. Sometimes your model has an area in which the polygons have gone wild—and I don't mean wild as in "Spring Break" wild. I mean the polygons are just not flowing correctly on your model and the smoothing is being affected. If your model is a mechanical object that was a frozen subdivision surface or a character face that needs repairs, then splines are your friend.

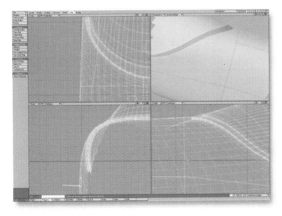

The easiest way to tackle polygons gone awry is to cut the offending polygons and place them on a separate layer. When you do this, try to make the object as square or rectangular as possible; that helps you when you build the patch. Try to make the area so that the sides have the same number of points on the opposing sides. In point mode, select a row of the points on the side of the area to be patched and make an open curve (commonly referred to as a *spline*) by pressing Ctrl+P. Do this for the remaining three sides (if you are doing one with four sides). Make sure you select the point in order and inline. Select the new splines and cut/paste them to a new layer.

With the splines on their new layer, select them in a counterclockwise or clockwise direction (depending on which way you want the polygons to face), but never cross sides while you're selecting. Call up the Make Spline Patch panel and change the Perpendicular and Parallel types to Knots. The numbers you use should be one less than the number of points on the sides of your patch. Click OK, and you should have a nice flowing patch that you can cut/paste/merge points back into your model. The points should match up perfectly!

   RELEASING THE POWER OF THE BRIDGE TOOL

LightWave 8's Bridge tool is great for connecting two sets of polygons, but did you also know that it functions as a great way to split polygons? If you use the Bridge tool while in Point mode, it acts as a super-powerful Split Poly. With Split Polys, you have to select the polygons you want to split, and then select the points to split the polygon. With the Bridge tool, simply select the points (no need to select the polys first) and use the Bridge tool. This saves one step that is required with Split Polygon.

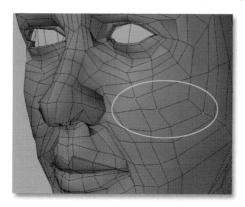 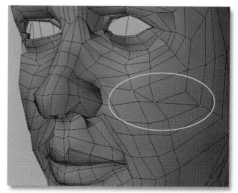

   FALLOFF CONTROL

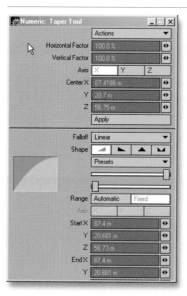

If you activate the Numeric panel while working with most of the tools under the Modify tab, there is a section for Falloff. Although there are subtle differences in the type of falloff you get, there are similarities, too. After you activate Falloff, you can jump through the basic operations using the arrow keys. Pressing the left or right arrows changes the falloff direction. The up- and down-arrow keys jump between the falloff shapes. That technique is quick, and nine times out of ten, using the arrow keys is a lot faster than having to make selections with the mouse.

BANDSAW—IT DOESN'T CUT WOOD!

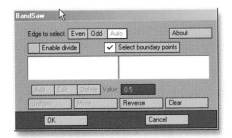

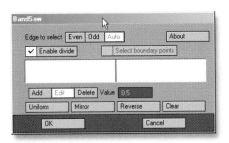

Slicing a path through your geometry by hand can be difficult. Luckily, NewTek provides a tool that makes this easier. BandSaw slices a row of polygons the way you define it, using its interface to direct its direction and location of the cut. It sounds confusing, but it isn't. The fastest way to use BandSaw is to select two polygons; the direction you select them defines the direction that you will "travel." Activate BandSaw and leave the Edge to Select at Auto. Click the OK button, and the polygons grow in the direction that you defined when you selected your first two polygons. Now cutting is done. Pretty slick, eh?

So now you want to actually cut something? Go through the same step, but when you get to the BandSaw interface, click the Enable divide button, and the last part of the interface will become active. The red line in the center represents the cut along the polygons. By default, it is at .5, which is 50%. Type in ".2" and you get 20%. A better way to describe it would be 20–80%. Click OK and watch BandSaw do its magic. It's powerful.

Watch out for a couple of things that can bite you. BandSaw only works with four-point polygons, so when it encounters a polygon that has a different point count, it stops its operation. Also pay attention to how your band of polygons "flow." If you want to examine how your selection will look before you cut, do it in Selection mode only (Divide disabled). Last, if BandSaw encounters a polygon that looks like a three-point polygon, but instead is a four-point polygon, it might cut the polygon mesh in strange ways. To avoid this, consider tripling the polygon first to stop the cut flow.

    DETAILS, DETAILS

It does not matter if you are making a short film at home for fun, making flying logos for the local car dealer, or working on the next summer blockbuster. One sure-fire way to balloon a scene to the point where machines start crashing on the render farm is to have too many polygons in a model. All too often, detail is added to models where it is not needed. If you have a small detail on a character—say a bullet that's in a belt clip and slung over the shoulder—it does not need to be a 24-sided cylinder. Eight sides would probably do just fine. Questions to ask yourself would be, "How close is the camera going to get to this?" "What will be the final format of my animation?" "Does this object play an important role in the scene?" "How will the final lighting affect this object?" If the camera does get close for a shot or two, consider making a high- and low-resolution version and using the high-res one for the few close-up shots. There are literally hundreds of questions you could ask. If something does not get very big on the screen, model smart. Make that object low in polygons!

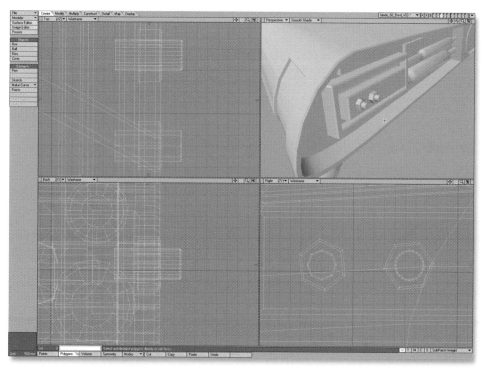

HEAD FROM A BOX?

One of the preferred methods for creating a head in Modeler is using subdivision surfaces. Although there are a wealth of ways to get started, the easiest is to use one of the primitives provided to you: the box, under the Objects heading on the Create tab (X). Most people would not think of this or might not believe it, but it is true. Create a head from a box, you ask? Read on… If you drag out a box in Modeler and activate the Subdivision surface mode by pressing the Tab key, it turns into a rough sphere. However, if you start adding detail to model your head, you will notice that it starts getting more and more box-like. To avoid this, freeze your box head. Under the Convert heading on the Construct tab (Ctrl+d), the box is frozen into a rough polygon sphere. You can then use this sphere as a polygon basis and press Tab to activate Sub-Ds again. This gives you much more detail to work with and avoids the tendency to pull back to a box. If you set the Patch Division (General Options) higher than 2, the frozen box might contain more polygons than you need, making the object difficult to sculpt into shape.

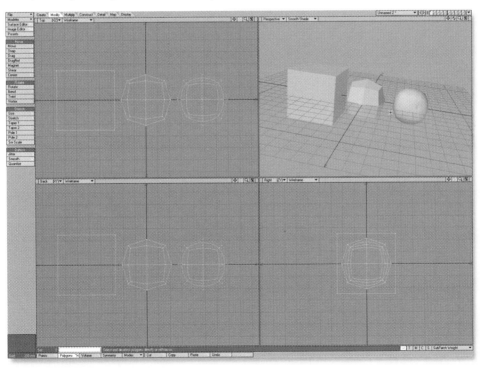

   WE'RE NOT CLONING DOLLY HERE!

If you have a tank and you need to make the treads, it can be quite distasteful to have to copy/paste/rotate into position and repeat for each segment of the tread. To make things easier, use the Rail Clone tool, found under the Combine heading on the Multiply tab. With your tread piece in the foreground layer and the spline defining the tread shape in the background, activate the Rail Clone tool. The best way to set up the tool is to have a knot at every location you want a tread piece. By adding the number of knots in the spline to the open field (by default, it's set at 20) and changing the Segments type to Uniform Knots, you will be good to go!

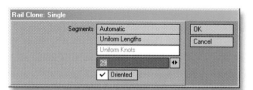

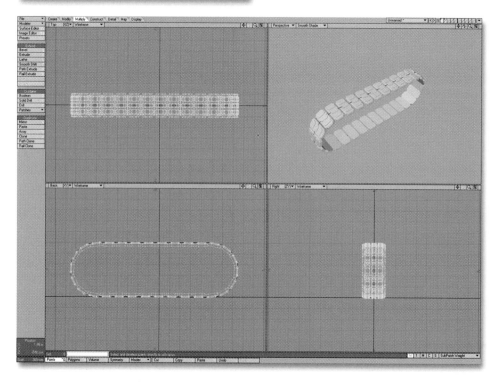

BEVELED WINDOWS

You can create the illusion of an interior for a sky-scraper in a simple and effective way without breaking the polygon bank. To do so, grab the polygons that will be the windows and bevel them in slightly; this creates the window framing. Then cut and paste the inset polygons to a different layer. Change their surface name to "Glass." Switch to yet another empty layer and paste again. This will be the interior of your building. Select all the polygons and bevel with Inset and negative Shift, which pushes the polygons back into the building. Don't go too deep, but don't go too shallow either.

Depending on how complex your building is, you will want to assign about five different interior surface names to these beveled interior polygons. If you were to keep their surface names identical, you might not have the control you want or need to create a window that holds up in the render. Again, it depends on your model size and complexity. The key to the effect is to change the Smoothing Angle to a high enough value that these interior polygons are smoothed. You do not want to see the bevel creases. With the surfaces defined for the interior, cut/paste them to the layer with the windows, and then cut/paste again back to the original building layer. Don't merge the points.

For surface attributes, give the window surface a glass look. You will need to give the surface transparency; after all, it *is* a window! For the interior surface(s), assign a complex-looking image map to each of the different interiors. The image map does not have to be of an actual building interior. My favorite ones are images from inside the International Space Station. Add a little luminosity (using the same image maps) so it looks like some of the rooms have lights on. Render away!

   SHIFTY CHARACTER

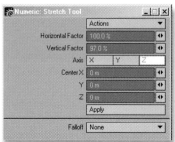

One of the best plug-ins available for Modeler is VertiBevel, mainly because of its capability to bevel a group of polygons in one operation. You can do this in LightWave, but it's a bit tricky. Select the polygons you want to bevel and use Smooth Shift under the Extend heading on the Multiply tab (F) to give it the shift you want for your bevel. This pushes out the group of polygons, away from its original location. Now switch your Action Center mode to Selection (Shift+F8). Using the Stretch tool under the Stretch heading on the Modify tab ("h"), stretch the selection inward to give the bevel its inset amount. You might want to use the Ctrl key to constrain the stretching if you only want it to apply on one axis.

A really fast way to do this is to use the new Super Shift tool under the Extend heading on the Multiply tab. Just select the polygons and use Super Shift. Super Shift is almost like an interactive bevel tool that works on polygon groups.

   BECOME ONE WITH THE CURVES

Merge Polygons (Shift+Z) is a great tool to use on polygons, but did you know it works great on curves as well? That's right! You can select multiple curves and press Shift+Z, and the multiple curves will become one.

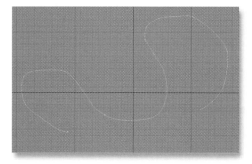 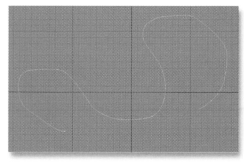

PRESTO CHANGE-O MOVE-O!

The Move tool can be used to move elements around in Modeler…duh! But did you know that you can convert the Move tool into the Magnet tool? Yup, that's right. Simply change the Falloff setting to Radial and presto change-o, you now have the Magnet tool functions. Changing the Falloff to Linear will transform the Move tool into the Shear tool. Experiment with Falloff and see what other surprises are in store for you.

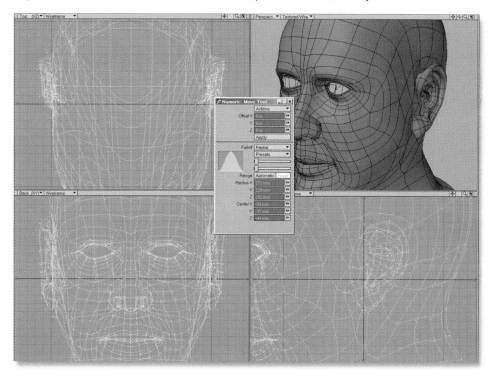

   ## 15 DEGREES OF ROTATION

Having trouble getting the exact rotation you want while modeling? Hold down the Ctrl key as you drag to rotate in 15-degree increments.

A TIME TO MODEL, A TIME TO SELECT POLYGONS…

So you've selected the points that are needed for your operation and realize that the tool you want to use only works with polygons. Before you succumb to frustration and drop your selected points, there's a new tool in LightWave 8 that was made for times like these. With the points still selected, choose Select Polygons from the View tab, and the polygons that relate to the points selected will be selected. Select Points works the other way around.

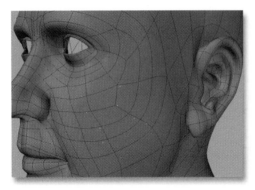
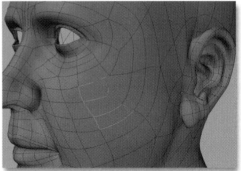

WELD POINTS WITHOUT THE DIRTY CLEAN-UP!

Using the Reduce Edges tool in LightWave 8 will accomplish the same task as welding points but saves you from having to select the two polygons you want to weld. The greater benefit to using this tool is that it won't leave behind two-point polygons like weld will.

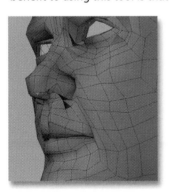

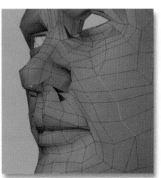

SELECT AND SAVE!

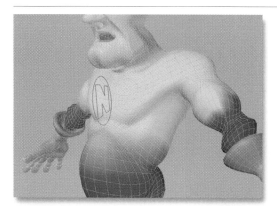

No, it's not a bargain bin ad. Select the polygons that make up the area on which you want to perform a Boolean or Drill operation. This will speed up the calculation and save you time. And, it really helps when working on high-poly objects.

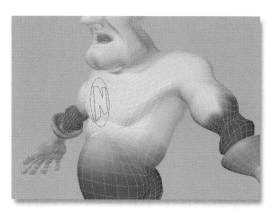

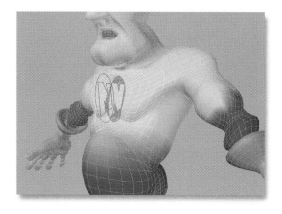

   THROW OUT THE IRON!

Wrinkles can add that extra detail that will help bring your model to the next level. Using the Edge Bevel tool introduced in LightWave 8 makes it super easy. Select the points that make up the edge you want to add the detail to and use Edge Bevel on it. To add multiple wrinkles to a forehead, simply apply Edge Bevel a few times, and then adjust the geometry until you're happy.

SPIN QUADS WILL FREE YOU!

This underused tool is more powerful than you might think. When you run into areas on your object where the polygons don't seem to flow right, Spin Quads could be the answer. Select the polygons that make up the problem area and click Spin Quads until the flow seems correct. Note: Clicking for the third time will place the polygons back to where they started.

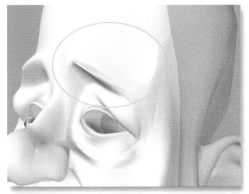 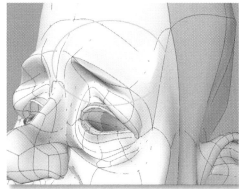

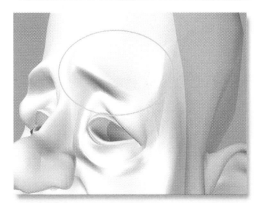 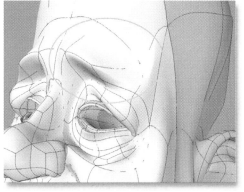

And God Said... Let There Be Lighting Tips

Caution–
Program
Deeper Than
It Appears

Lighting. It's yet another important piece of the CG puzzle. LightWave does it so well. Come on! Look at the name of the package. It's not called RenderWave, ModelWave, or ParticlesWave, now is it?

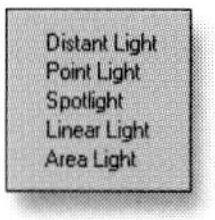

Distant Light
Point Light
Spotlight
Linear Light
Area Light

And God Said

Let There Be Light—Lighting Tips, That Is

Lighting is a critical part of making your scene look professional. The best modeling, animation, texturing, camera work, and so on will be destroyed if your lighting is less than perfect. Part of perfection is learning to use the tools that are available to you. And you don't just need to know how to use them— you need to know how to use them well, and how to use them effectively and efficiently. Getting to know your way around and learning to use the tools to their fullest is not that difficult. Here are a number of tips to help you on your way. Let us show you the light.

   LIGHT FALLOFF MEASUREMENT FORMULA

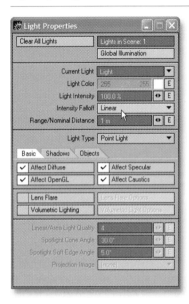

Lights in LightWave are on a permanent sugar high; they just keep going, and going, and going, kind of like 2-year-old children. But maybe you would like your lights to behave a little more like they would in the real world? That would be nice, wouldn't it? Say, for example, that you have lights parent to an auto-mobile as headlights. In the real world, the farther the light is from the subject, the dimmer the lights are. Without a falloff setting in LightWave, those head-lights would always light the subjects, no matter how far away they were. To calculate a light falloff, all you need to know is this: A 20% light intensity with a 50% falloff goes 0.4 meters. With that said, light intensity, divided by the falloff percentage, equals the distance in meters traveled. Of course, you can't apply falloff to a distant light because that type of light always shines, like the sun.

   USING FLARES INSTEAD OF LIGHTS

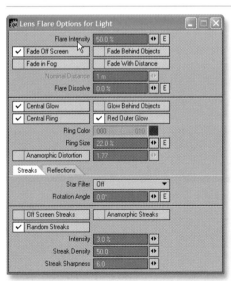

Rendering's a pain, ain't it? And complex lighting scenarios don't help much. But here's one tip that can give your system a boost. To help LightWave calculate render times, use a lens flare to simulate lights that are in the distance or that are not really lighting anything. After all, they aren't just for cheesy 1980s logos! Use a lens flare to represent a light source. Be sure to take the intensity down to 0 and turn off shadows to speed up render times. Work smarter, not harder!

TOO MANY LIGHTS? JUST RENAME THEM…

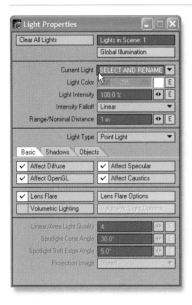

Lights in LightWave 3D are just cool. Why? Because you can turn on as many as you like without your wife or mother yelling at you! You're not wasting electricity at all! You are, however, going to waste time trying to decipher which light is which after they're added. Instead, just open up the Light Properties panel, and then select and rename Current Light. That's it! LightWave 8 allows you to quickly and easily rename lights directly in the panel.

GLOW BEHIND OBJECTS

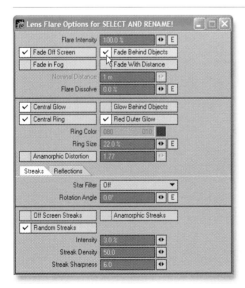

Whenever you use Glow Behind Objects in the Lens Flare panel, remember that the flare light source should always be positioned behind an object. If the light source resides within an object, the flare cuts through the object. A common mistake when you're first using lens flares is to leave Glow Behind Objects on when you don't want it on. We've seen our fair share of demo reels with blinking landing lights on spaceships. They look great when the flares are unobstructed by a part of the ship. However, when the spaceship turns and the flare burns right through—yup, you got it—Glow Behind Objects was left on. The demo reel is ejected and filed in the cylindrical file cabinet.

   BETTER SHADOW MAPS

Ah, so you figured out the quick way to create shadows, did ya? Shadows maps can only be applied with spotlights, and they're rendered from memory, rather than from the system processor. This makes shadow maps ideal for quick rendering over ray-traced shadows. But you know, sometimes the quality is just bad, right? Are these artifacts and jagged edges from shadow maps getting you down? No worries, mate. The trick is to go wide and tight. That's right—wide and tight. Simply make your cone angle really wide, such as 60 or 70 degrees. Then move that light close to the subject, and your troubles will subside.

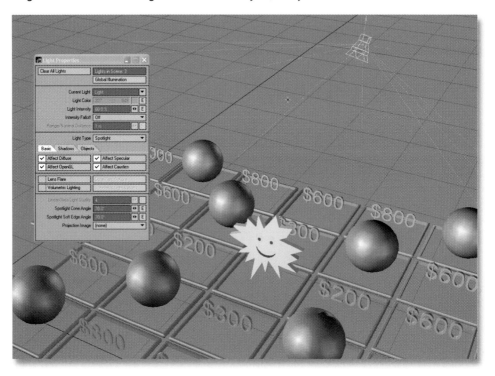

SOFTER SHADOW MAPS

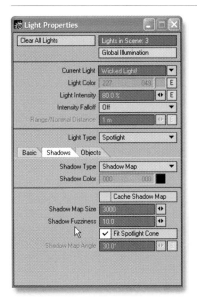

Now that you understand how to eliminate the jaggies that are so common to shadow maps, how can you make them softer? Hard-edge shadows are so 1980s! Head on over to the shadow map portion of the Lights panel, and change the default shadow map size from 512 to something like 3,000 or more. But be careful—setting this upward of 12,000 or more might bring your system to a screeching halt. See, this is a memory setting, and increasing the value tells LightWave to use more memory for the particular shadow. After that value is jacked up, you can increase the shadow fuzziness for a softer-edged shadow.

   FUN WITH NAMES

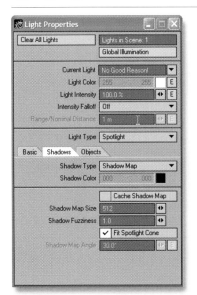

When LightWave renders shadow maps from spotlights, the render display shows information as "rendering shadow map for x light." You can rename a light to something like "no good reason" so that your render display will show "rendering shadow map for no good reason." Why would you do this? Well, for no good reason, really. You could do it just for fun, and it's more fun when you put a scene together for someone else. When your friend renders, he's in for crazy hilarity and hijinks! Oh! So much fun! (Note sarcasm.) Thanks to Mr. Steve Bailey for this great tip many years ago!

   ## WHAT THE HECK DO LIGHTWAVE LIGHT VALUES MEAN?

Because LightWave's light settings don't actually represent real-world specifications, what do they mean? Are they just arbitrary, or a secret code? Certainly not! Say that you have an object that is light blue, RGB value 0, 200, 200. And say that you had a 0% ambient intensity and a 100% value set for Diffuse in the Surface Editor. With these values, the render would display the exact color of the object: 0, 200, 200. Now, say that you changed Light Intensity to 50%; your rendered objects pixels would be 0, 100, 100—half their original color. By the same token, if you changed the diffuse surface value to 50%, the results would be the same because you're telling your object to only take half of the light source intensity. If you added a 10% ambient intensity, your color values would now be 0, 220, 220. 10% of 200 is 20—hence, the new 220 value. Your object is now 20% brighter. See? It all makes sense now.

   ## COPY AND PASTE LENS FLARES

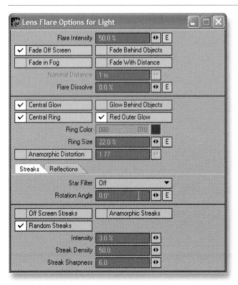

Sometimes you just don't want to put on all those settings for every single light; it's such a pain. But there is hope, young Luke, because you can copy and paste lens flares without issue. When you apply a lens flare to a light from the Light Properties panel, just make sure that the panel is active, and press Ctrl+c to copy the settings. Then use your up arrow to quickly select the next light (assuming you have more than one light in your scene), and then press Ctrl+v to paste the lens flare values. Be sure, though, that you have the Properties panel back into focus. (This means that you have to click on the panel again.) The real benefit of this is to keep your lens flares consistent while saving time.

DETERMINING LIGHT FALLOFF

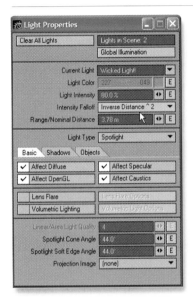

Yeah, yeah, Light Falloff. You get it, we know. It's easy, right? Wrong. How do you know how to set it? Is there a quick and dirty way to actually see what you're doing, rather than calculating yet another value? Sure, there is! If you put on the Intensity Falloff in the Lights Panel, and then go to an orthogonal view in Layout, such as Top, Front, or Side view, you'll see a falloff ring around the light. Simply adjust the Range/Nominal Distance in the Light Properties panel, and interactively change the falloff value without guesswork.

MULTILIGHT CHANGES

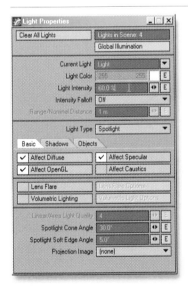

So you have a scene with a ton of lights and the client just called you on the phone to tell you he needs to have an update soon. The update requires you to update 124 lights—all with the same settings. You've lost most of your hair already, so you really don't want to start ripping more out. Luckily, you can now update all the lights as if they were one. Just multiselect all the lights that you want to change, open the Properties panel, and change what you want. All the lights update with the settings you selected. Now you can make that hair replacement appointment.

OBJECTS AS LIGHT SOURCES, PART 1

Have you ever needed to make an object a light source? You know, you have a big gold urn that your character is gazing into, but you want that urn to emit light and color? You don't want a light shining out of it, but rather, you want the object to be a light? A great way to do this in LightWave is to turn on Radiosity from the Global Illumination panel, which is located within the Light Properties panel. A good example of using this technique is using big, flat, white luminous polygons as light sources. These polygons with Radiosity turned on will work like a light box in a real-world photo studio. The radiosity will spread or "diffuse" the color of that polygon onto other polygons in your scene.

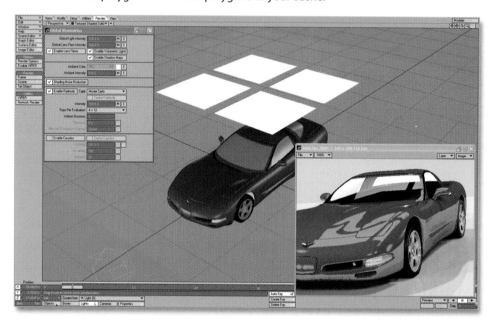

OBJECTS AS LIGHT SOURCES, PART 2

Radiosity? Who's got time for that? Well, if you do, that's just great. Good for you. But have you ever wanted to create lights based on areas of an object rather than the object itself? Say, for example, that you want to create a disco ball that emits light. Instead of creating dozens of lights and then parenting them to your 1970s throwback object, go into Modeler and select the polygons you want to emit light. Then, under the Setup tab, beneath the Layout tools, select Add Luxigon. LightWave will ask you what type of light sources you want to have created for the selected polygons, and you can choose the intensity, shadows, and color. Next, in Layout, choose the Convert Luxigon command and whammo! You're John Travolta.

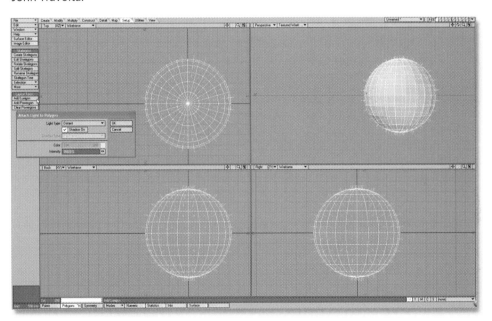

   FUN WITH GOBOS

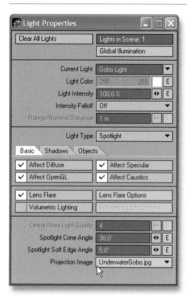

You can use one gobo, or cookie, on a light in LightWave. Traditional studio lighting folks know that these little gems can help give a dull set some life. With LightWave, you not only can put still images onto spotlights, but you also can put moving images there. On a simple level, make a black-and-white image in an imaging program such as Adobe Photoshop. Make sure six white squares are on black, and blur them slightly. Save out the image and load it into LightWave via the Image Editor. Then open the Light Properties panel and make the light a spotlight. At the bottom of the panel, you can specify a Projection Image. Choose the image you made, and then focus the light onto a set or object and press F9 to render. Your light now shines through those white boxes, and the black areas block the light. Another cool thing is that you can actually *see* this in OpenGL within LightWave to get instant feedback while setting it up! Talk about a time saver!

Taking this idea further, you can use a black-and-white image of leaves to simulate light coming through trees. You're not limited to black and white, either. You can take a full-color movie if you like and project it onto other objects, simulating the look of a movie projector or slide machine. If you happened to make an underwater texture from Chapter 8, that rendered black-and-white movie can be projected onto a scene to simulate the underwater caustics of a pool or ocean. Cool stuff!

GRAINY RADIOSITY? NO WAY!

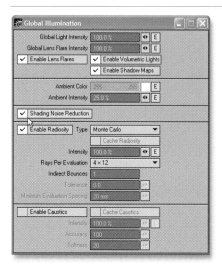

Radiosity is cool, no question. But render times are just brutal! Even after you wait for that sucker to render, the image quality is poor and grainy. There are two things you can do to fix that right quick. Go to the Radiosity settings within the Global Illumination panel. You can get there through the Light Properties panel. In the middle of that panel is a little check box named Shading Noise Reduction. Turn that on to diminish your grain. The other sure-fire way to fix that grain is to increase the Rays Per Evaluation setting for the radiosity. A good preview value could be 3×9 or 4×12. Test your renders with these settings. Then, when everything is the way you like and you're ready for the final render, set that value to 12×36 or higher. You'll have longer render times, of course, but you'll also have better-quality renders. And, leave the Shading Noise Reduction turned on, even in the larger final renders.

AMBIENT LIGHT—USE WITH CARE

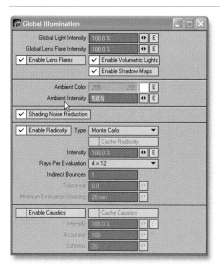

Deep within the Light Properties panel, under the Global Illumination settings, a small value named Ambient Light exists. By default, this setting is 25%. *Ambient light* is the area in your LightWave scene that is not directly hit by a light source. This 25% value is too high for most situations. Bring this value down to about 5% or even lower. The areas that are hit by light will appear brighter, and the areas that are not hit by light will appear darker. If you need more light, add it, but don't rely on Ambient to do the job for you. Ambient flattens out your scene and pulls contrast. Of course, you might want this type of look, and if so, ignore this tip.

MAKING CUSTOM RADIOSITY

Radiosity is the crème de la crème of 3D renders. It's realistic, believable, and hard to control. People often take radiosity as a replacement for 3D lighting; although you can do this, there is a better way. The best way to use radiosity is with LightWave's existing light structure. For example, you're creating a sweet new corvette ad. You put it on a set, light it with standard area lights, and away you go. Now, instead of adding more lights as "fill" lighting, turn on radiosity to have the model take on diffuse lighting from the rest of the 3D scene such as the set, or big, flat, white luminous polygons that act as soft lights.

COOLER AREA LIGHTS

Area lights are the most realistic light you can use within LightWave. These types of lights mimic a studio light box and create accurate realistic shadows. But sometimes after you've added the area light, you realize that the shadow is not that soft. What many people aren't aware of is that you can increase the size of the area light. Select the light, and then from the Items tab, select Size from the toolbar on the left side of the Layout interface. When you increase the size of the light, your shadow becomes softer while retaining accuracy.

BAKING RADIOSITY

Radiosity is cool, no doubt. But if you're just doing an architectural fly-through, there's absolutely no reason to allow LightWave to calculate radiosity for every frame. Instead, bake it in! Create a UV map for your entire object in Modeler. Then in Layout, turn on radiosity, and go to the Surface Editor to add the Surface Baker shader. Double-click the newly added Surface Baker entry and set the parameters, and don't forget where you saved the baked image. Press F9, and you'll see the Baking in Progress panel appear. When that finishes, you can press Esc, turn off radiosity, and then load that baked image. Simply apply the baked image to the UV map you created for the entire object's surfaces, and you'll have the radiosity image mapped onto the polygons.

As an extra tip, turn up Ambient Light, sometimes to 100%, in the Light Options panel to make the image maps fully visible.

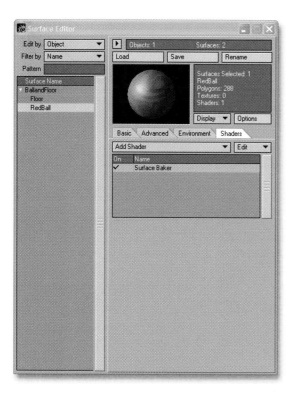

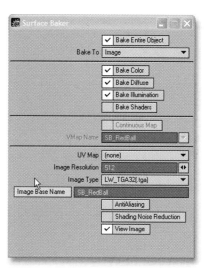

   3-POINT LIGHTING—A STARTING POINT

What is 3-point lighting? It's an industry-standard "default" lighting setup that works well for many things in LightWave. You can use this setup for character, product shots, and even medical animations. The formula works like this: Set a "key" light to the top left or right front of the 3D set. This is your brightest light. Then add a light that is half this brightness to the opposite side, and make it an off-white color—even blue if you like. This is your "fill" light. Finally, add a "hair" or "back" light behind the subject to separate from the backdrop (some-times called *rim light*). This back light can be bright or dim, depending on the subjects' surfaces. From here, you can tweak and add more lights as you see fit.

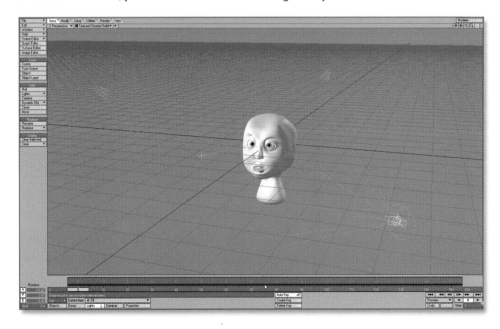

MULTILIGHT KICKER

What's cool about LightWave is the fact that you can mimic the real world in 3D, especially when it comes to lighting. One thing that lighting directors often add to a set is a kicker light. This light adds necessary fill to the side of an object, for example. With LightWave, you have no wires or bulbs to worry about, so you can add more than one light as a kicker and change the colors of each, creating a cool, complex multilight kicker.

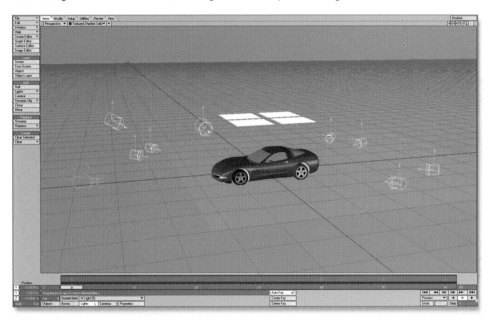

  EXCLUDE LIGHTS QUICKLY

Tired of selecting each light that you want to exclude from an object in the Object Properties panel? Right-click on the Exclude Light bar to bring up the pop-up window and quickly select all the lights or clear all selected lights. The Invert Selected option is a quick way to select lights as well. This new feature to LightWave 8 is a great time-saver.

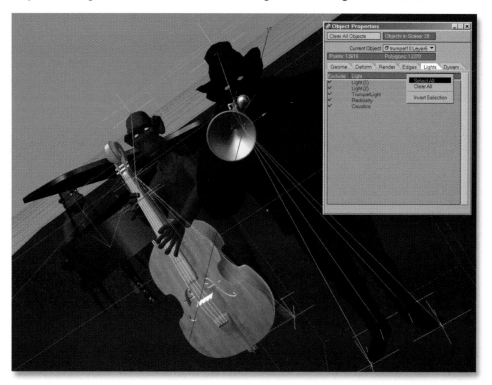

Keep Moving On

Bright Lights Ahead

A great animation is never completed; it is merely abandoned.

Dope Sheet

Keep Moving On

Motion Tips for Movers and Shakers

It does not matter if you are animating a complex character of a simple bouncing ball; there is a lot more to animating than just setting keyframes. After you have the basic timing down with the keyframes, you can start massaging your animation by manipulating the keys and their relationship with every other keyframe. Understanding this is critical. The tips in this chapter are here to make your life easier so that you can concentrate on bringing your animation to life and stop wondering where the life-support machine is because you can't figure out the software!

   COPYING KEYFRAMES IS EASY!

So maybe you've created this complex character and set up precise movements, and suddenly you realize you need the same settings at another point in time. What's an animator to do? No worries; it's easy to copy keyframes in Layout without using the Graph or Scene Editor. Simply select the layout item you want to set a keyframe for, and then go to the desired keyframe you want to copy. Then press the Enter key on the keyboard, and a requester called Create Motion Key pops up. In the numeric entry is a value that represents the current keyframe. All you need to do is enter in the new keyframe and click OK (or press Enter). You've now copied the current item's keyframe.

   CLEAN MOTION BLUR

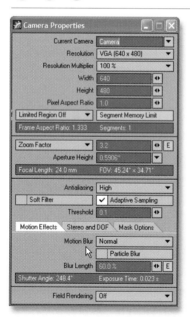

Sometimes you just need that realistic look. You know—fast blurring images! If the image is too clean, it looks too much like computer-generated imagery, and we can't have that. So, add motion blur to your scenes. When you add motion blur, make sure that you get a good clean blur, not just staggered images. In the Camera panel, when you turn on motion blur and set Blur Length to say, 60%, be sure to increase the Antialiasing setting to High for the cleanest motion blur.

ADD MASS AND WEIGHT TO KEYFRAMES

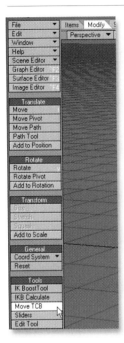

Have you ever noticed keyframes? You put a couple of them together and they act all goofy? That's because keyframes in LightWave create curves. And, like Illustrator or another program that creates art with curves (Bézier, for example), the other points around the art determine the shape of the curve. In LightWave, you can open the Graph Editor and adjust individual keyframes to have varying effects. If you apply a bias to your keyframes, you can add more mass and weight. Say that you have a car whipping around a corner. Instead of just making the car turn the corner, slap some bias into that keyframe and watch the car fishtail. You can quickly do this in Layout by going to the Modify tab and using the MoveTCB tool. Select the tool, and then interactively adjust Tension, Continuity, and Bias values in Layout. You can see your adjusted values in the information area at the bottom left of Layout.

   QUICK CAMERA ZOOM

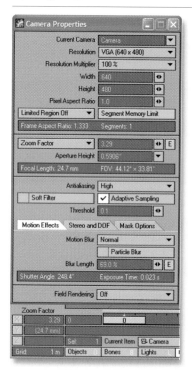

It's darned cool that you can mimic real-world cameras in LightWave, but sometimes it's a real pain to open the Camera panel, find that Zoom button, and make the change. Ugh! Instead, select the camera you're using in Layout and press the "Z" key. Yes, "Z" is for zoom—how original! Then click and drag. It's an instant zooming camera! What's more, you can go to a new keyframe, zoom the camera, go to another keyframe, zoom the camera again, and so on. You just avoided using the Graph Editor to set varying zooms!

ADJUSTING KEYFRAME VELOCITY

Perhaps your style isn't fishtailing cars around corners. You're so difficult! Alrighty then. Let's say that you like your keyframes to have a little more motion, a little more style. Set some keyframes, perhaps for an animated amusement park ride, and then in the Graph Editor, add continuity to your keyframes to add some wicked velocity. (Continuity enhances a change in the object motion path. Most of the time, you will be using negative values.) This can affect how your item moves in and out of the key. And, don't forget that you can use the MoveTCB controls in Layout as pointed out a couple of tips ago. (Continuity is using the right-mouse button and dragging up and down with the mouse!)

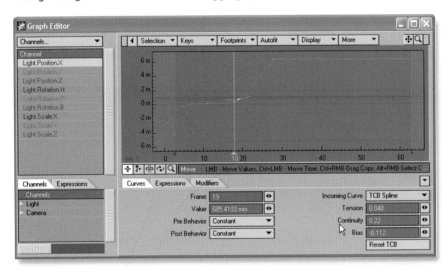

    EASY DOES IT!

If this is all too fancy for you, and you just want to have an item ease into a keyframe, you can do that, too. It's something that every animator should know: how to ease in and ease out of keyframes. Make your objects slow down and rest, rather than abruptly stop. Or, on the flip side, you might want your object to move faster into a keyframe, like a bouncing ball. Just open the Graph Editor and apply a tension of 1 to ease into a frame (which flattens the curve toward the keyframe) or a value of –1 to slam into a frame (which tightens the curve around the keyframe).

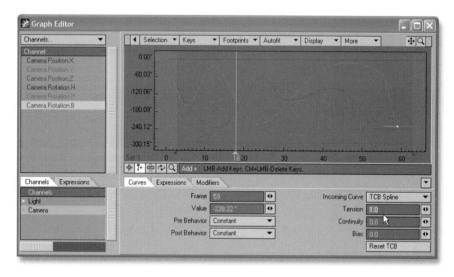

FOLLOW THE LEADER

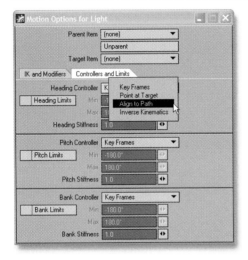

Follow the leader! No, I'm not talking about the game, but rather a tip that can help you make your items follow a motion. For example, say that you made the coolest tunnel ever, and have used the same path that created the tunnel for your camera motion. But you realize that although the camera moves through the tunnel, it doesn't actually follow the path. Well, if you've already loaded a motion for your camera, you can press "m" for motion options in Layout and select the Align to Path option for either the heading or pitch. Your camera twists and turns accordingly. Where do you get the motion path? That's simple; just create a curve in Modeler, and then use the Path to Motion export control from the File drop-down menu.

  BAKE YOUR CURVES

Working in the Graph Editor can be confusing. But what's worse is when you make adjustments to your keyframes when you don't want to. What a mess! Instead, select the channel you want to edit; then, from the Keys drop-down list at the top of the Graph Editor, select Bake Selected Curves to freeze the selected motion curve to lock that sucker in place.

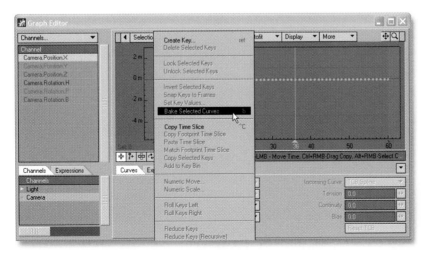

   INSTANT ENDLESS ROTATION

So, get this: Your client has a brilliant idea. Don't they all? He wants you to create a seamless loop of his logo for 10 minutes. "Sure!" you say. "No problem!" But then you calculate how long 10 minutes takes to keyframe and render out on your 500Mhz computer, and you start to sweat. But wait…. Don't sweat! You can make one short animation and loop it as long as you like! All you need to do is rotate the object over a set number of keyframes, and make sure the last frame is the same as the first. Then open the Graph Editor and select the rotation channel you keyframed. At the bottom, under the Curves tab, select Repeat for the Post Behavior. Now you can render as much as you need and then loop this animation in your favorite editing program.

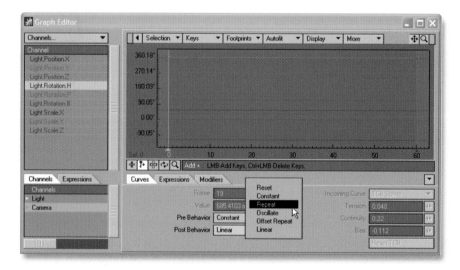

WHAT'S YOUR FOOTPRINT LOOK LIKE?

If you're animating something complex, such as the next great purple dinosaur, open the Graph Editor and leave a footprint for your fcurves. Why is this a tip? Well, it can work as sort of a master undo for your animation. It works well to counter Layout undos. Just be sure to have the fcurves visible within the Graph Editor, and you can take a step back when you want!

Not many people know that if you leave a footprint and then delete all the keys, the footprint will still be there. Place the cursor over the frame that you want a keyframe for and press Ctrl+b. It drops the keyframe that is snapped to the footprint. This is one of the best uses of footprints.

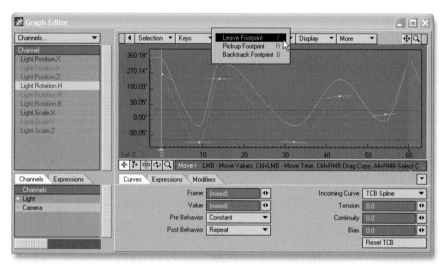

  ### X MARKS THE SPOT!

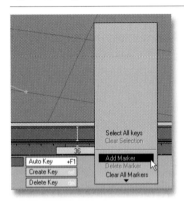

Well, it's not really an X, but let's say that you're creating the next major million-dollar blockbuster animated movie. And your timing needs to be just perfect. But before you commit, you might want to remember where you were going to place the proverbial next step for your character. Use LightWave 8's Dope Track to add a marker. Move your bone or rig control into the desired position; then in the Dope Track at the bottom of Layout (click to open above the timeline), right-click where your timeline slider is, and select Add Marker.

   ### LARGE KEYFRAME POINTS

Argh! Those damn little keyframe points in Layout are just too hard to see! I keep selecting them when I don't want to, and I miss the ones I need to select. There's got to be a better way! There is. Open the Graph Editor, and click the Options button at the top of the screen. Click the Display tab within the panel that opens. Click on Large Keyframe Points and fix this nasty problem. Oh, and while you're there, change the color of those keyframes, too!

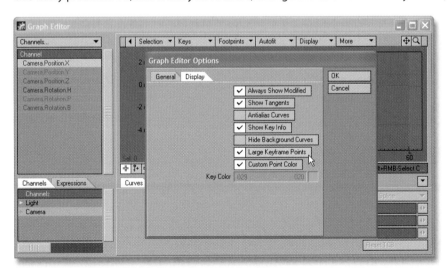

TRACK LAYOUT ITEMS

Have you ever noticed how annoying it is to select an item, open the Graph Editor, make changes, close the Graph Editor, select a new item, and then open the Graph Editor again to edit? Wouldn't it be nice to have your selections automatically update in the Graph Editor's channel bin? You can do that! Open the Graph Editor, go to the Display panel drop-down, and click on Track Item Selections. With this, you can leave Graph Editor open all the time. Then every time you select a different item in Layout—be it an object, camera, light, or bone—its channels are automatically available for editing in the Graph Editor. Time is money!

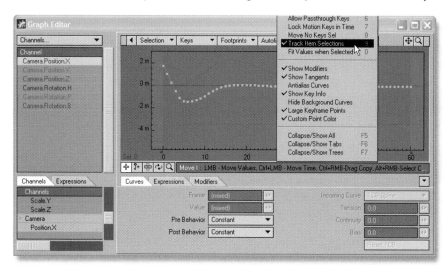

    KEEP YOUR SEATBELTS FASTENED!

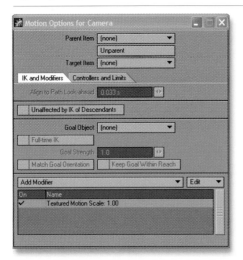

Not that we're poking fun at earthquakes or anything, but it's really cool to make one in 3D. It's easy, too. Did you know that? Have you ever tried keyframing something like an earthquake? Faahghetaboutit! Open your favorite scene. Select the camera, and then press "m" for Motion Options. Find the Textured Motion plug-in from the Add Modifier drop-down list. Double-click the plug-in after it's loaded, and then click the Texture button. Make Layer Type Procedural, which calls up Turbulence by default. Change Turbulence to Underwater, and then click the Play button in Layout and watch your camera shake around like a bag full of beans! Now add variations of this to the X and Z channels for extra coolness.

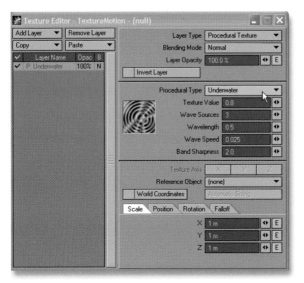

SUPER-COOL SPLINE DEFORMATION

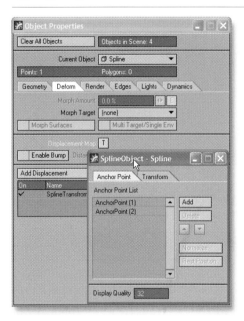

All the tips in this book are within LightWave. However, every once in a while, you need to go beyond the software. You need— the Internet. And if you go to http://www.shift.gr.jp/html/staff/sp/sp000003.html, you'll find a free, cool-ass plug-in called Shift Spline Transform. After you add it to Layout, this plug-in is easy to use and allows you to quickly and easily animate an object down a path of your choice. This is cool for snaking objects or ropes. And, did we say it's free? Yeah, it's free.

  QUICK RE-TIME MULTIPLY KEYS

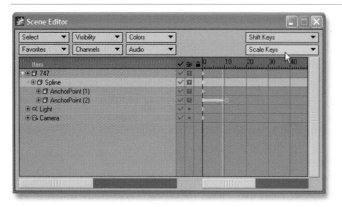

You have that animation looking so sweet. Hundreds of objects are perfectly timed, and you're in love with yourself. Then your client comes in, and he's now in love with you, too! But then he asks you to make it two seconds shorter. He doesn't see that as a problem—it's only two seconds! Argh!

Nightmare! You need to redo all the keyframes! Or do you? Open the Classic Scene Editor, and click the Scale Keys button. Here, you can globally change the timing of your entire scene, or just selected objects. Scale Keys multiplies.

   QUICK RE-TIME ADD OR SUBTRACT KEYS

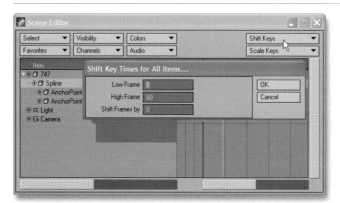

So maybe your client isn't that picky, and he just wants a few items to last a little bit longer onscreen. It's still going to be work for you to change these keyframes. But then there's the Shift Keys option in the Classic Scene Editor! Click this little sucker to add or subtract keyframe values from your selected items or your entire scene.

To do this in the new Dope Sheet, select the item channel you want to offset, right-click on it, and select Numeric Offset under the Selection heading. When the window opens, type in your offset value, click OK, and you're done! Or, even easier, you can simply drag the items in the Dope Sheet to the location you desire.

MOVE ALL KEYFRAMES

Let's say you've made the most excellent broadcast logo animation the world has ever seen. You've spent countless hours perfecting it, only to realize that the main logo enters at completely the wrong time. Its motions are perfect, but it comes into frame too soon. Well, instead of rekeyframing it entirely, just shift its motions. Create a new Scene Editor instance, select the item in motion, and on the right side of the Editor panel, click and drag around the keyframes. Next, click and drag to move all the keyframes simultaneously. By the same token, you can click and drag on any of the actual keyframes in the Scene Editor and change their position in time quite easily. Just click and drag.

This also applies to the new Dope track; select what you want, and drag to a new place in time. It's easy as pie. Well, to be honest, it's a lot easier. Have you ever tried to make pie? It's not that easy!

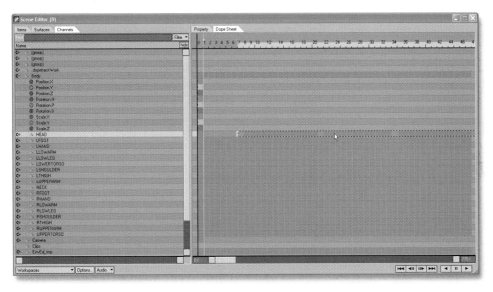

COPY MOTION PATH

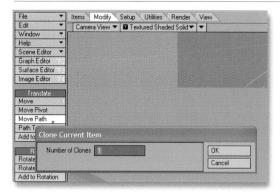

It's time to animate the Chicago Air and Water show! You take your best Stealth Bomber model and whip it across the city skyline. It twists and turns and rotates as it passes low over the crowd. You now need another plane doing the same thing, with just a slight delay. You can do this without keyframing a second object. Just select the original keyframed object and press Ctrl+c to clone as many as you want. Then select the desired cloned object, and from the Modify tab, select the Move Path tool. Click and move the entire motion path for the cloned object. All keyframes are retained but moved to a new location. You can then open the Scene Editor and shift all the keyframes slightly for a little delay by dragging the keyframes a bit. You can repeat this process quickly and easily to create a full formation of airplanes, or anything else for that matter.

ANIMATE TO SOUND!

Character animation in LightWave 8 is easier than ever, no question. But sometimes, you simply haven't a clue what to do with your character. Here's a tip that's really more like common sense. Animate to sound! All the professional movies you see are done this way, so why not do yours the same way? Just open the Scene Editor, and from the Audio button at the bottom of the panel, load a WAV file. You'll see the audio spectrum appear in Layout's timeline. Now scrub your timeline and move your character to the sound. Remove the guesswork! Oh yeah, and turn up your volume!

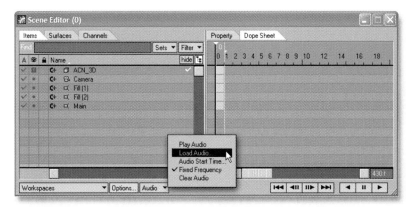

     COPY THE KEYFRAME, YOU DOPE (SHEET)!

Although Dope Sheet is a bit of an odd name, there is nothing dopey about it. For example, if you select keyframes in the Dope Sheet, you can copy them to a new location while leaving the originals behind. Select the keys you want to copy, hold down Alt, and left-click and drag them to a new location. It's fast and easy, just the way you like it.

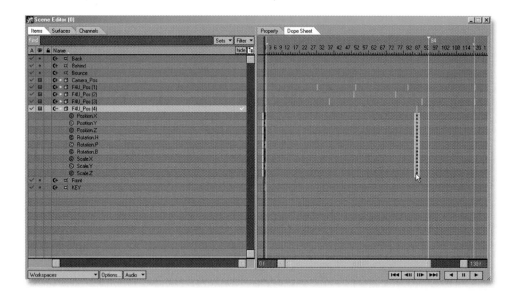

FOOTPRINTS IN THE SAND…ER, GRAPH EDITOR

When using motion capture data, every frame has a keyframe and doing edits can be a mess. Use Footprints in the Graph Editor to help clean up the motion files. Select the channels you would like to clean and choose Footprints/Leave Footprints. Delete all the keyframes, and you will see that the footprints are ghosted in the editor. Use the Match Footprint to TimeSlice (Ctrl+b) command to drop keyframes that match the Footprints. It's an easy way to clean up the keyframes but get the same motion.

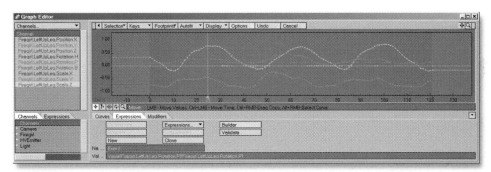

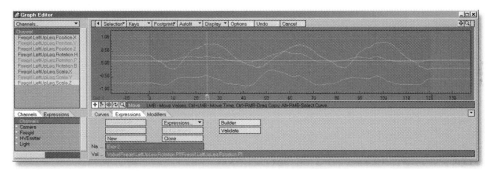

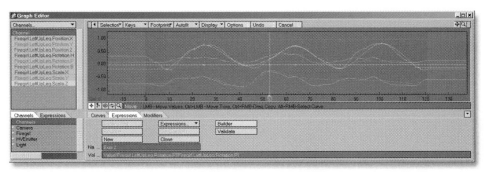

   MOTION MIXER MASTER CHOREOGRAPHY

Motion Mixer was designed to bring the same concepts found in non-linear video editing to computer animation. You can store, re-use, and adjust motions for entire hierarchies. You can even mix motions together. But did you know that you can share motion files between actors? That's right—just make sure that you have the same rig structure and naming conventions, and you will be able to share motion files between characters. With LightWave 8's Import/Export RIG format, this becomes much easier than before.

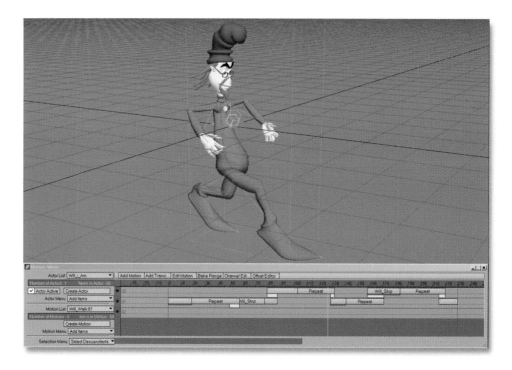

MARK YOUR TIMELINE TERRITORY

LightWave 8's Dope track adds all sorts of great new functionality to the timeline. Dropping markers on the Dope track can be a great way to keep track of important frames in time. If you want to set a keyframe for multiple items, simply drop a marker and it will show up for all items in the scene. Dropping a marker is very easy—just right-click on the frame you want and select Add Marker.

  YOU ARE NOW ENTERING THE BAKE ZONE

The Dope track is great for editing keys for the selected item, but you can also quickly add groups of keyframes easily with Bake Zones. Hold down the Alt key and click and drag the left mouse button to place a Bake Zone. At any time you can right-click within the zone and choose Bake Current Zone. Baking Keys is very handy when you use IK in an animation but need to output to a game engine that doesn't support IK.

   WHEEL OF FORTUNE

If you have a mouse wheel, you're in luck. When you select an object in layout, use the middle mouse wheel to switch between move, scale, and rotate functions. If you don't have a mouse wheel on your mouse, never fear—the spacebar on the keyboard will do the same thing. This beats selecting the same modes on the Toolbar.

MAKE PATH, NOT WAR

Make Path will make your life easier! Dynamics in LightWave have never been more power-ful! Use the Make Path command located under the EditFX tab to create a Null object that has the same motion path as a specific point on your dynamic object. A great use for this command is to place a particle emitter on a specific point of a tire that has a flat. The emit-ter will match the tire's movement perfectly.

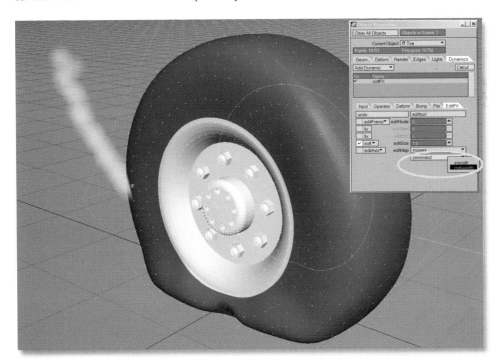

What Gets Under Your Skin?

Keep Moving

Bones are one of the most powerful tools to have ever hit the CG world.

Faster Bones

What Gets Under Your Skin?

Skeletal Deformation Tips

Character animation changed dramatically when bones became available to the average consumer who had a desktop computer. NewTek has taken bones a step further—no, a leap forward—than what they were before. This enables the character rigger, animator, and setup people to take bones to a whole new level. The ability to split bones, heal bones, and export entire rigs for reuse are tools that will save you an enormous amount of time. Bones—they aren't just for character animators, either!

  BONES FOR MECHANICAL ASSEMBLY

People too often confuse LightWave's bones for stupid things like character animation. What bones are really good for are mechanical assemblies! Okay, they are great for character animation, but you can also use bones for mechanical assemblies to perform operations such as swinging arms, rotational pivots, and more. To do this, you can make one simple object, rather than objects made up of multiple parts. Instead of parenting all those separate object parts together and then setting up some messy inverse kinematics, just use bones! The only thing you need to do is make sure that the parts needed to be animated are cut first and then pasted back down, without merging points. Then just weigh each part and specify each bone for each weight.

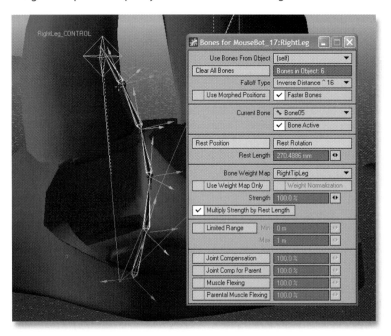

AVOID BONE ROTATION PROBLEMS

Creating bones via skelegons in Modeler is a great way to work. But too often, clever animators rig their characters in multiple views. This is bad, Grasshopper, bad. Why? We're so glad you asked. See, when you draw a skelegon in a face view and then make the child bone in another view, the base rotation is changed. What does this mean? Basically, it means that when the skelegons are changed to bones in Layout, one bone will rotate on what you think is the pitch, whereas another might rotate on the pitch for heading, and another might rotate the bank for the pitch. Confused? Don't be! Just make sure that when you're building skelegons in Modeler, you create them all in the same view, such as the back/front view. Then use the Drag tool to move and position them into place.

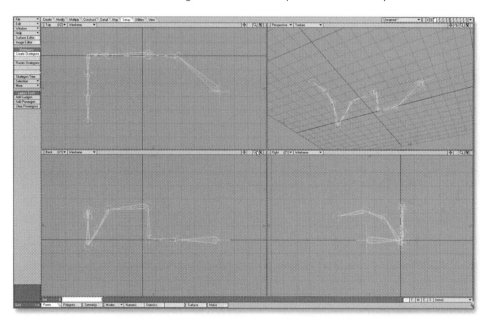

  THE HECK WITH MODELER—FIX IN LAYOUT!

Let's say that you weren't quite awake when you created your skelegons in Modeler, and you don't want to have to load the object back in, change the bone rotations (also known as Bone Up tags), and then convert them again to bones in Layout, and so on. No problem! In LightWave 8 Layout, under the Setup tab, select the Bone Twist function. Then, as if you haven't already figured it out, twist the bone! You'll want to do this in the bone's original resting position.

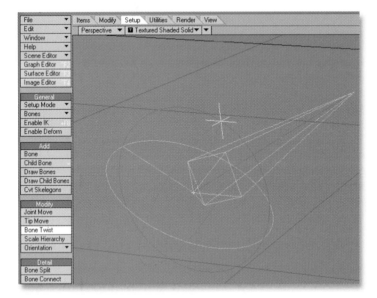

With all these cool bones tools in Layout, you might find yourself spending less time in Modeler using skelegons. Yea!

CLICK AND HOLD!

Have you ever created skelegons in Modeler, only to convert them to bones and suddenly have your object disappear? Yeah, us, too. But here's what's happening. Most people tend to do a quick little click as they begin to build the skelegons in Modeler. They first select the Skelegon tool, click in a view, and then click and drag. That first little click actually creates a skelegon! When you activate skelegons in Layout, the bones deform the object, as they should. But that teeny tiny bone created from the quick click sizes down the object to nothing, making your object sort of disappear. To avoid this, make sure that when you're creating skelegons in Modeler, you select the Skelegon tool, and then click and hold and drag! Do not let go until your skelegon is created.

Hint: You can always use the statistics window (w) to see how many skelegons you've created and then count them. So, where you think you see three bones, statistics shows that there's four! If there's an extra skelegon you can't actually see, you've got one of those teeny tiny ones!

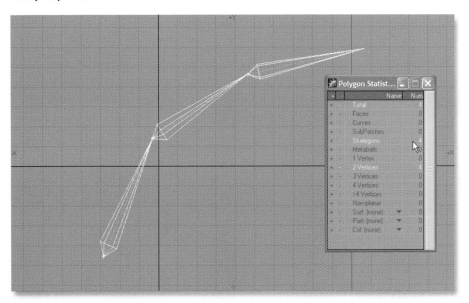

   BOOST THAT IK, BABY!

LightWave 8 has this slick little tool called IK Boost. To use IK Boost, simply select the object with bones applied to it (or converted from skelegons). Then go to the Modify tab and select the IK Boost tool. Click and drag on the root of the character, and guess what? You just applied IK to your entire rig! Make sure you set constraints, though; otherwise, it could get messy—very messy. Now, there are many more things you can do with this killer tool, so read on.

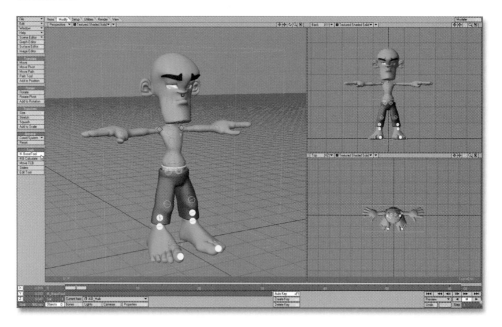

TIME TO FIX WHAT MIGHT BE BROKEN

Sure, Inverse Kinematics is cool, and you've quickly and easily applied it to your character with the IK Boost tool. But having IK on your entire object doesn't always mean that you have complete control. At times, you'll want to fix the IK. To do this, right-click on the base of the bone you want to fix. Then select Fix. This is much like the "fix" setting in dynamics.

   BAKE IK MOTION

As fast as LightWave is, some things just get you down. No, not your taxes, but the time it takes to calculate certain motions is just too darned long! So, bake it in! That's right—LightWave 8 not only lets you bake in textures, but it also lets you bake in the IK motion. When you're running IK Boost, open up the Dope track above Layout's timeline (just click in the center of the bar) and then right-click and drag on the timeline the area you want to "bake" and select that option. This is a great option for gamers. Many game engines do not read IK. To get around this, use IK, but then bake it out!

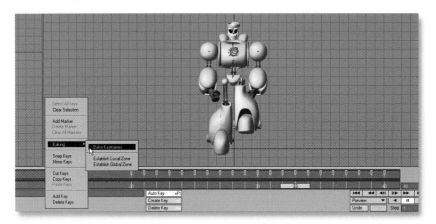

   CONTROL GRAVITY

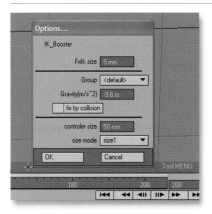

Using the super-cool new IK Boost in LightWave 8, you can now fix, or lock, the gravity on bones. Just open the options for IK Boost and fix the gravity. This instructs the bones to have gravity, which in turn affects the objects.

GIVE THAT BONE A HAND!

Give that bone a weight, actually. Give that bone a hand just sounded better! Anyway, have you ever wanted to deform an object without the messy hassle of keyframing IK? Apply bones to an object. Then activate IK Boost, and you can right-click and instantly set weights and dynamics on bones. These dynamics tell the bone how to react to various effects. If you are familiar with Motion Designer or the new dynamic settings, then you should feel right at home with the new bone dynamics. But, unlike regular dynamics, bone dynamics make keyframes. Because bones are deformation tools, the bones deform the object accordingly. What this means is that adding a simple wind effecter now blows your bones about like sticks! For example, if those bones are attached to a tree, your tree branches are now blowing in the wind.

QUICK! EDIT THE LIMITS!

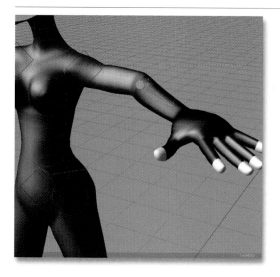

Those crazy bones just want to do their own thing, don't they? Often, rotating bones just has them bending too far and deforming your object beyond your vision. Instead, activate IK Boost, right-click the desired bone, select a bone, right-click on a particular channel, and select Use/Set Limit. Then select Edit Limit to enter the limits you want to use. A quicker way to set limits is to hold the Ctrl key and click and drag that channel to the position you want the limit to be. When you undo the move, the limit is set. This helps those unwanted movements and keeps your bones in line, so to speak.

BORROW SOME BONES

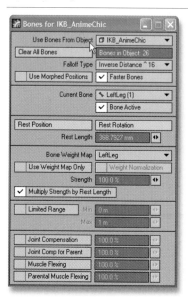

Now that you've figured out how to go to a new layer and create some killer skelegon rigs in Modeler, you can't seem to get them to work in Layout. The reason for this is that bones need to be part of an object to deform that object. If the bones live on another layer, even within the object set, they still won't work. Or will they? All you need to do is select the object you want to deform. Click the Bones button at the bottom of Layout, and then open the properties for those bones. At the top of the panel, select the Use Bones From Object command and choose the layer where the bones reside. Now those bones affect the current object. Note that you can have other objects in your scene be affected by other bones in the scene with this command.

DON'T BREAK A BONE

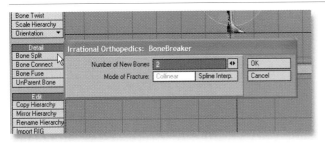

Even if you spend an enormous amount of time setting up bones for a character, you might soon realize that some bones are just too big. Perhaps you only made one long bone for an arm. How is the arm going to bend? Maybe you put one bone in for a finger and then realized you need three bones instead. Rather than ripping apart the rig and resetting everything, simply use the Bone Split tool to split that bone into as many as you like, while retaining the hierarchical structure. First select the bone to be split, and then go to the Setup tab. Click Bone Split and set the appropriate values. What's really cool about Bone Split is that it retains all the settings, such as weight maps applied to the original bone. That way, you don't have to redo them. Bone Split does the work for you.

   MIRROR, MIRROR ON THE WALL

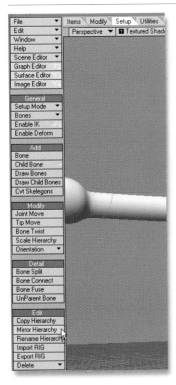

Setting up bones is not so hard, but it doesn't have to be time-consuming, either. That way, you can have more time to eat and sleep, don't you think? If you create a set of bones, a hierarchy, or even a null (!) in Layout, you can quickly mirror them. This is great for characters that are symmetrical, such as donkeys. Don't worry about duplicating your work; just select Mirror Hierarchy from the Setup tab and go.

CHAPTER 7 • Skeletal Deformation Tips **145**

  BE A HEALER

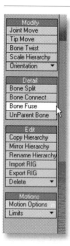

So, a few tips ago you got tough and started to break some bones. Who ya workin' for, huh? Well, as things turn out, you really need that bone to be whole again. Man! There's no pleasing you! Well, that's easy enough to fix without going to the emergency room. Simply select the desired broken bones and use the Bone Fuse tool from the Setup tab to join two bones into one. It's quick and easy, and there's no bill from the doctor.

   OH, MY JOINTS!

Bones are great; bones are cool. However, every once in a while, the joints of these bones need to be adjusted. Before LightWave 8, this was pretty hard to do. Okay, we lied. It wasn't possible. Yes, we know, you can't believe it—a flaw in LightWave! But in case you need to adjust those aching bone joints to move their pivots so that they rotate the way you want, you just use Joint Move, and you'll be all set. Left-click and drag on the joint to move it. If you want to move an entire hierarchy, then use Tip Move, which works like Joint Move, but on an entire hierarchy. LightWave 8 is great. Yes indeedy.

USED BONES, GET THEM CHEAP!

How many times have you wanted to reuse a hierarchy for a character? Why re-create a rig every time you have a new character? Well, after you have a rig in Layout, you can export and import it back, with the new RIG format making bone setup a lot easier. All praise LightWave 8!

GET IN LINE!

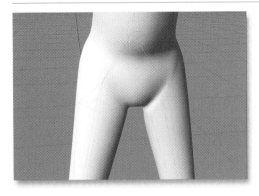

If you use bone twist on a bone in a bone chain and get the Bank rotation just the way you like it, why not cheat on the remaining bones in the chain? With the bone still selected, simply choose Align Pitch, and it will apply the same setting to the next bone in the chain; you can repeat until you're all the way down the chain. Aligning the Pitch rotation has never been easier.

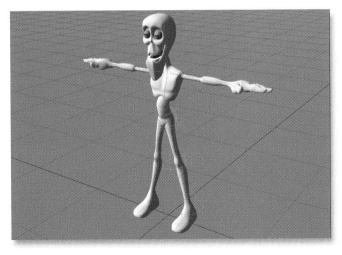

   BONE BREAKIN' GOODNESS

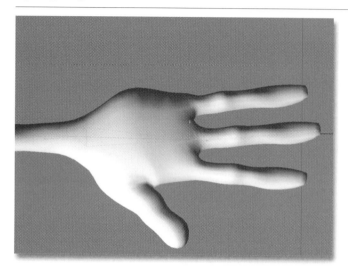

Bone split can save you time when placing bones. Let's take a hand, for example. Draw one bone for a finger and apply all the settings you would normally use (such as Weightmap). Choose Bone Split and change the number of new bones to 3. Ta da! Your finger is fully boned. This works great for spines, legs, and arms as well.

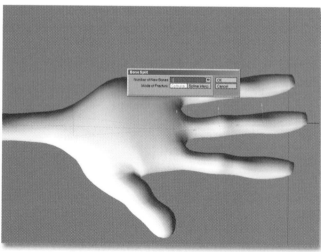

DEAD MAN'S CURVE

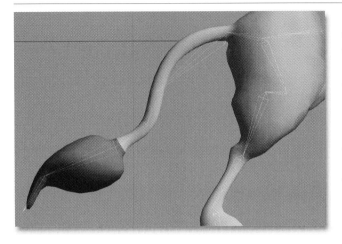

Placing bones on a curve couldn't be easier now that we have Bone Split in LightWave 8. Just like we did earlier when placing bones in a finger, place one bone on a curve. Use Bone Split like we did before, but this time click the Spline Interp. Option. Voilà! The curves will flow on the curve between the two bones. It's magically delicious.

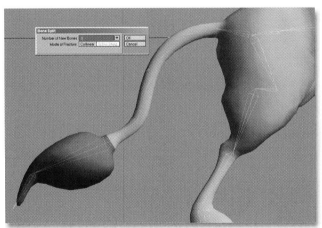

CHAPTER 7 • Skeletal Deformation Tips   **149**

   ## THE POWER OF BONE PLACEMENT

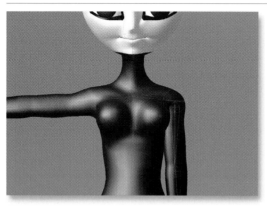

Not all mesh deformations need to be tweaked with weight maps. A common problem area for character deformations is the shoulder area. Selecting the shoulder bone and moving its end with the Joint Move tool to help support the shoulder geometry could do the trick and doesn't involve you going back to Modeler to tweak or add a weight map. This also works great in the butt and hip area.

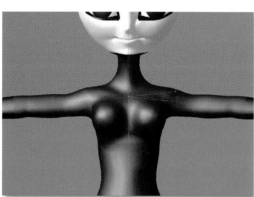

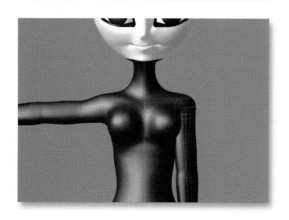

SIZE DOES MATTER...

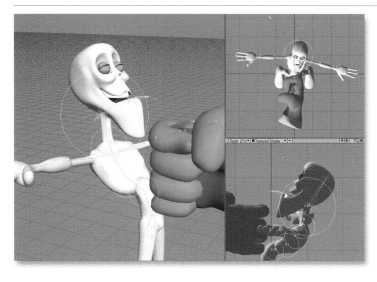

...especially when working with Bone Dynamics with collision objects. If you want to ensure that the collision object doesn't pass through the geometry of the object with IK Boost applied to it, simply change the size of each bone to encompass the mesh. If all bones will have the same size (a snake would be one example), change the Key Edit Mode to "All Items" and any changes you make to one bone will be set for all bones.

ONE SELECTION TO EDIT THEM ALL!

OK, so that was a bad "LOTR" reference, I know. Instead of selecting just a few bones to edit using Bone Twist, Joint Move, Tip Move, and Scale Hierarchy, select the object that the bones are in and choose one of these tools. You will be able to edit every bone in the object. This is great for when you have many adjustments to do.

Beauty Is Only Skin Deep

Skeleton Crossing Ahead

Ah, yes. Beauty is most certainly only skin deep. The nice thing about LightWave is that we get to set just how deep that is!

Beauty Is Only Skin Deep

Surface and Texture Tips

With so many powerful tools available to us in LightWave, it is easy to lose sight of the basic operation that really sets LightWave apart—one of which is its wonderful surfacing and texturing ability. All the options available to you, the user, are just a few clicks away, unlike some of the other packages that give you carpal tunnel syndrome when you try to add the most basic surfaces. So sit back and enjoy being a little shallow for once— because sometimes beauty really is only skin deep.

  WHERE DID MY SURFACES AND SETTINGS GO?

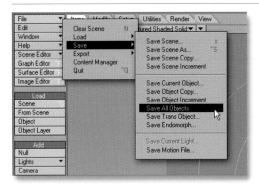

It's probably happened to you, too. You work hard on making the perfect model. Then you spend hours and hours texturing it, tweaking it, and getting it just right. Great! All done. Then you come back the next day and load up your most perfect scene, only to find that your object is suddenly sent back in time and has no surfaces at all! Who did this? Is this a sick joke? Actually, it's not anyone's fault. You just need to learn one thing: Save All Objects! That's it. Surfaces are saved with objects. Saving the scene saves motions, light setups, camera moves, and anything else associated with the scene. Use the Save All Objects command from the File drop-down to save your surfaces to your objects.

If you are working with Cloth FX, Hard FX, Soft FX, and so on, you need to save them as well. They are not saved with the scene automatically; you need to make sure that you save them. After you execute the save, LightWave automatically loads the file into the Load field when you load the scene. To save, open the _FX panel, go to the File tab, and click on the Save Motion button. That saves the motion to a file (which will be used from there on out to deform the object).

FAKING CAUSTICS

Every once in a while, you'll need to create that cool underwater refracted caustic look. You know, those cool cycling patterns that dance all over the ocean floor? Okay, maybe they just crawl on your pool walls, but whatever. Here's how you can create those cycling caustics on your pool walls without the need for true caustics. Oh, what's wrong with true caustics? Um, do you have like two years for rendering? Stop asking questions and read on.

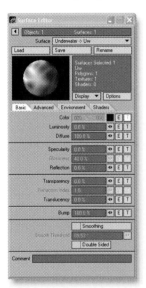

Make a flat polygon in Modeler and bring it to Layout. Square up the camera on the polygon so that it fills the frame. Then go to the Surface Editor and make sure the surface color is black. Click the T button for Color to apply a texture. Select Procedural Texture for Layer Type and Underwater for Procedural Type. Change the size (bottom of the panel) of the texture to about 20m for X, Y, and Z. Then set Wave Sources to 10. Adjust Wave Speed to fit your needs of speed; something like 0.0115 is good. Set Wave Length to about 0.5. Open up VIPER from the Render tab in Layout and make an animated preview with it. You should see cool moving underwater patterns. Render this out as a sequence or movie file. Then load that movie back into LightWave when it's finished and texture map it onto the walls of your pool as a transparency map (which is why the surface of the object was black). Or, better yet, apply that movie to a spotlight as a projection image. (See the "Fun with Gobos" tip in Chapter 5.) You can project the moving underwater pattern to swimming fish, scuba divers, or mermaids in your scene.

What? You want the texture to loop? Jeez! Okay, read the next tip.

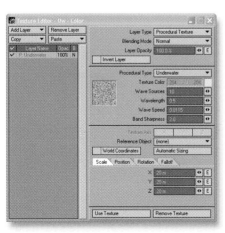

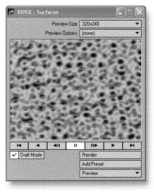

 SEAMLESS LOOPING TEXTURES

This is a killer technique for making lengthy cool looping backgrounds. You can render this out, make variations, render that out, and keep doing this for the next four weeks. Sell all of these and retire young. Here's how it works: Go to the Window drop-down list in Layout at the top left and select Backdrop Options. From the Add Environment selection within the Backdrop Options, double-click Textured Environment. Then click the Texture button that pops up beneath. In the Texture panel that appears, set Layer Type to Procedural. Select Underwater for Procedural Type. Also, open VIPER from the Render tab in Layout to see what your results will look like. (You'll need to do a test render once the Viper window is open; otherwise, you won't see your updates.) For Wave Sources, choose 3. Now, here's the

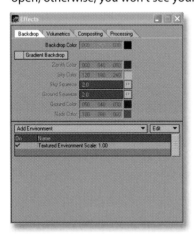

formula: Wavelength divided by the number of frames (such as 60) gives you the proper wave speed to make a perfect loop. So, with Wavelength set to 0.9, divided by 60 frames, Wave Speed should be set to 0.0015. To enhance this further, increase the size of the procedural texture on the Y-axis, and maybe rotate it a bit for variation. Make another layer on top of this one by just copying it and pasting it down. Then vary the new layer with a different color and speed. Keep doing this until you're completely exhausted. Oh yeah, press F9 to see what this looks like rendered. This texture renders in LightWave's background, in case you haven't figured that out.

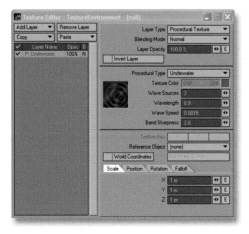

INSTANT ELECTRICITY FORMULA

Did you ever sit down on a breezy Saturday afternoon and think to yourself: "Hey, I need to create some cool electricity?" You can use this cute little formula to create instant electricity for crazy storm clouds, freaky characters with super-duper powers, or even for a laboratory experiment. All you need to do is apply a procedural marble texture to a flat polygon. Increase the Frequencies and Vein Sharpness values to create an electrical bolt. To animate this, simply apply a value to the Z channel of the position. Because you're applying this texture on a flat polygon, the Z movement makes the texture come alive.

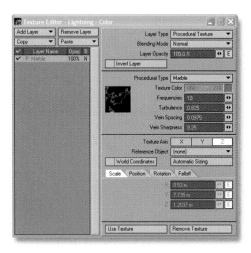

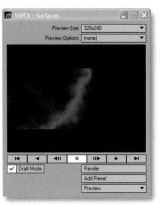

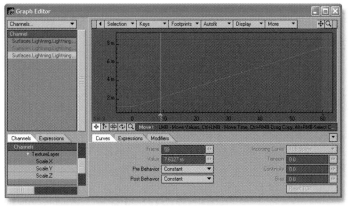

    THE GRADIENT GAME

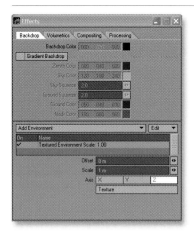

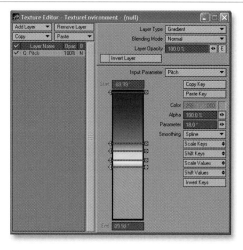

You might think that the gradients in LightWave are too complicated to learn, right? Bzzzzt! Wrong! Thank you for playing! Even though we could write a whole chapter on working with gradients, this tip will give you the "ah-ha" you've been looking for to figure out those pesky gradient strips. Understand that the way the gradient bar in the Surface Editor is laid out (vertically) has absolutely nothing to do with how the gradient is applied. What determines how the gradient is applied is the Input Parameter, which by default is set to Previous Layer—not what you always want, so be careful. The Input Parameter tells the gradient how to be applied, such as on the bump map channel, if a bump map is applied to the same surface. Also understand that the gradient bar works from the bottom up. Say, for example, that you're surfacing a sunset. The deep orange color starts at the bottom of the gradient strip. The lighter orange is above that, there's light blue for the sky, and there's a deep blue for the higher altitude. Setting the Input Parameter to Pitch angle produces a killer sunset. You can use the Texture Environment plug-in within LightWave's Backdrop panel to apply this to the background in Layout. What's more, you can layer variations of turbulent procedural textures on top of the gradient to create clouds. It's an excellent and fast alternative to Sky Tracer.

DIFFUSE SHARPNESS—OXYMORON?

We think not. Diffuse Sharpness is an odd setting buried within the Advanced tab of the Surface Editor that used to be labeled Sharp Terminator. How weird is that? This setting is pretty useful when it comes to setting up shading where the difference between light and dark needs to be more defined, such as on a planet. Planets are generally lit more dramatically, with the lit side bright and the nonlit side dark, with little gradation between.

 ## ADDITIVE TRANSPARENCY IS MORE TRANSPARENT?

Another odd name for a cool setting, Additive Transparency is also found within the Advanced tab of the Surface Editor. This tricky little setting takes the color of the background in a scene and adds it to the color of the surface. If your surface is black, the surface appears as transparent because the background values are applied to the 0,0,0 surface color. So why is this useful? How about a fireball explosion or flames from a rocket ship? Additive helps blend these surfaces with the background color.

    FAKING REFRACTIONS

Refraction calculation in LightWave is significantly faster than any time in the past. However, it still can be a real render hog. Let's say that you need to make an object float across the screen underwater as you're looking down at it. Obviously, the object would appear bent under the water due to the refraction, right? Well, if you've applied an animated displacement map to make the water wave, simply cut and paste the water's displacement map to the object's displacement map. Instead of having LightWave calculate true refraction, simply deform the object with the same procedural pattern you are deforming the water with. No refraction needed! Just make sure your object has been properly subdivided so that it can bend easily.

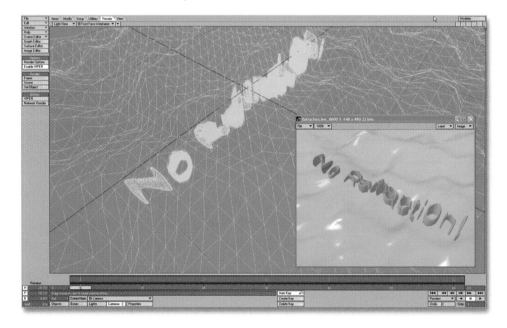

MAKING SURFACES WIREFRAME

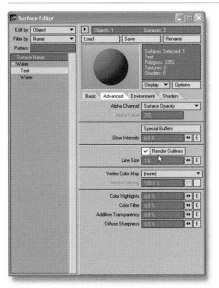

Every once in a while, you'll need to render something as a wireframe. You know, that cool animated heads-up display you've been making? Or perhaps you're knocking out some cool architectural style animations. To make your object's surface a wireframe when you click the Render button, just go to the Surface Editor and select the desired surface(s) you want to make wireframe. Then select the Advanced tab and click Render Outlines. After the wireframe is active, you can set a Line Size for it. Usually 1 or 2 (pixels) is good. Because this is done on a surface-by-surface basis, you can make an entire object a wireframe, or just parts of it.

TEXTURE ANTIALIASING—A GOOD THING?

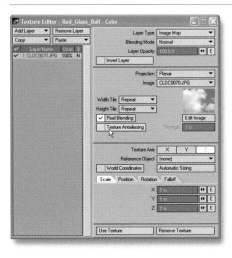

Antialiasing is the process of smoothing edges for a cleaner render. Generally, you would turn on antialiasing in the Camera panel for your final renders. But wait! Why is there Texture Antialiasing within the Surface Editor when an image map is applied? Is this a good thing? Not really. See, antialiasing is really a blurring to soften edges, or pixels. If you turn on Texture Antialiasing and then render your animation with antialiasing, you'll end up with blurred textures. Turn off Texture Antialiasing for most image map situations. However, you might choose to keep it on for bump map textures because this blurring is a bonus for smoothing out bumps.

  CARTOON-STYLE SURFACES

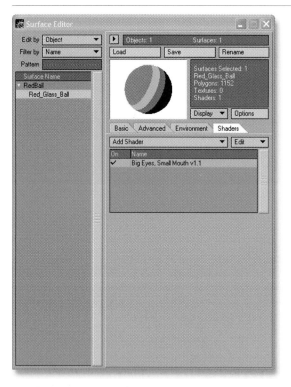

It's really, really stupid to think that you would want to take a powerful, fully functional 3D application to make a flat 2D render. What is this world coming to? Well, you're the boss, so follow these steps: Go to the Surface Editor and select the surface you want to turn into a cartoon. Then click over to the Shaders tab and click Add Shader. Select the AH_CelShader plug-in. When you render, your object will be shaded like a cartoon! You can step up the look of this render by using the BESM plug-in. BESM means Big Eyes, Small Mouth, which gives you sort of that Japanese Anime look.

BESM is more complex and gives you more control over the surface settings. Another add-on you can apply is turning on the edges for the object in the Object Properties panel. Within that panel, click on the Edges tab and turn on all the edge attributes for your object. Doing so creates that familiar cartoon outline around your object. Last, from the Lights and Global Illumination panel, bring Ambient Intensity up to about 50% to flatten out the lighting. Voilà! 3D cartoons.

SURFACE THICKNESS FOR EASY DEPTH

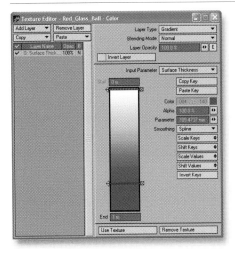

If you happen to be making a nice little pond in one of your 3D masterpieces, you might be interested in this cool, little-known feature in LightWave. Surface Thickness is a setting found when you apply a texture gradient from the Surface Editor. Say that your pond surface is colored a nice and murky blue. Click the Texture button for color, and make Layer Type a Gradient. Set Input Parameter to Surface Thickness. Add some keys to the gradient, and you can control the visible depth of your pond. This feature also works great for surfaces such as marble and human skin and can be a great fake for SSS (the fancy way of saying subsurface scattering).

FRESNEL (FRE-NEL) EFFECTS

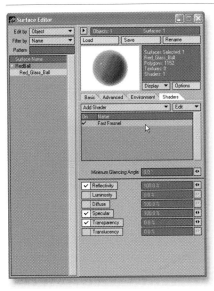

The first thing you should know about Fresnel effects is that the *s* is silent. If you're going to use a tool, know how to pronounce it! This setting is a Surface Editor shader that you can add to simulate more real-world lighting situations. You can choose from two shaders: Fast Fresnel and Real Fresnel. Fast Fresnel allows you to control reflectivity, luminosity, and many other values, whereas Real Fresnel gives you control over specular and reflective polarization. So what do you use Fresnel effects for? Well, have you ever walked up to a car window, and as you got to the car on an angle, you could barely see into the side windows? Because of your angle to the windows, your eye sees more of the reflections in the window. But as you come closer to the car window and stand in front of it looking straight in, it's much easier to see through the glass. The reflection is not quite as strong. This "glancing angle" is the Fresnel effect. Add this shader to glass, car paint, metals, or any other surface that can benefit from controlled glancing angles.

  SMOOTHING ANGLES

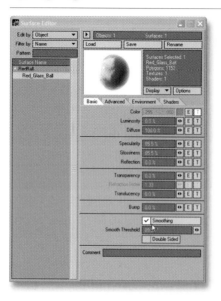

For some crazy reason, when you click on the Smoothing option for a selected surface within the Surface Editor, it defaults to 89. In most cases, this is way too high. For example, if you have a logo with a front, bevel, and side surface, putting smoothing on the side and bevel with this default setting creates too much of a rounded look. Any reflections will render poorly, and it will look like your logo has an error of some sort. Because the front of your logo is flat, smoothing is not needed. Turning Smoothing on will create unwanted results. This smoothing option is a Phong surface shading that visually changes the facets of your polygonal models. A setting as little as 20 is often just enough for proper smoothing.

   MANIPULATING THE PROCEDURAL TEXTURE WINDOW

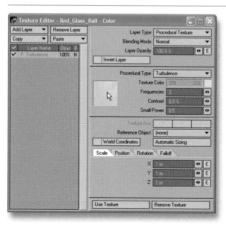

Get into LightWave and apply a procedural texture to an object. Any object will do. You can do this by clicking the T button in the Surface Editor for Color. Make the Layer Type Procedural, and the default Turbulence texture will appear. You can change the colors, the size, and so on as you see fit. But, in case you chose a color that makes the tiny thumbnail texture preview hard to see, all you need to do is right-click on it and choose a new background color for the preview. Another thing you can do is click with the left mouse button and drag Procedural view around to see how the pattern thumbnail looks.

SURFACE PRESETS ON THE FLY

So you've worked on a surfaces setting for quite some time and you want to save it to the Preset Shelf. Easy enough…simply double-click on the Preview sphere in the Surfaces panel, and it will appear in the Presets panel automatically.

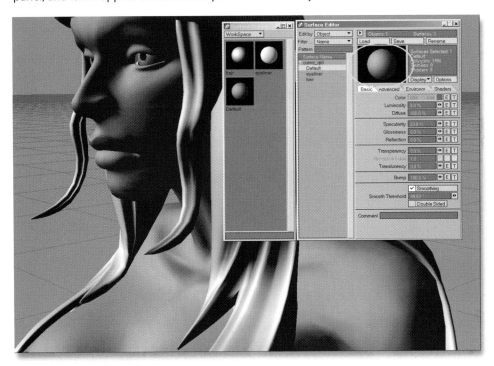

You think you have it all set up and ready to go; the animation is complete, lighting is just perfect, models are beautifully

Render Status

Get Out! Just Get Out!
Rendering and Saving Tips

made, and textures are so nice they would make da Vinci jealous! So now it is time to start rendering to see just how it all looks and observe that hard work transformed to beautiful pieces of art. It is not always as easy as just pressing a button to get that perfect render. These tips are here to help guide you through some of the pitfalls and ensure that you get what you want—the first time!

   ADAPTIVE SAMPLING—WHAT'S THE DEAL?

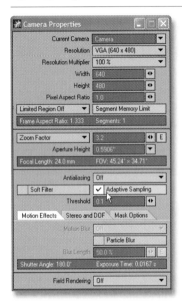

I bet you're wondering just what this render setting does? Located within the Camera panel, Adaptive Sampling helps clean and speed up the render process. Perhaps you need to get your renders cooking faster, and really, why wouldn't you? Turn on Adaptive Sampling, which makes rendering more efficient by performing edge detection on the first render pass of images. Anywhere additional edges appear, additional render passes occur. Any non-edge pixel, such as in the middle of an object, only gets one pass of rendering. Because antialiasing is only necessary for pixels that make up the edges of objects, Adaptive Sampling eliminates unneeded computations.

   CROSS THE SAMPLING THRESHOLD

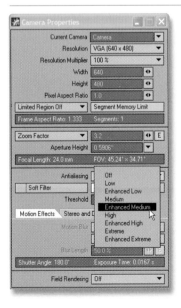

Perhaps you liked the previous tip? Good! We're glad that you do. But after you turned on Adaptive Sampling, another little button popped up, didn't it? How would you make your render times go even faster? Simple—adjust the Sampling Threshold! This quick little value setting located in the Camera panel just beneath Adaptive Sampling is an edge detection algorithm (that's really smart math) that determines how different neighboring pixels must be for edge detection to occur. A higher threshold value, perhaps 20, significantly speeds up the antialiasing process of a render pass (that will make rendering faster), but has less edge detection. A low setting, perhaps 0.1, takes a little longer to render but has greater edge detection. What you choose to use depends a lot on the scene. Start with the default and increase the number by small increments until you reach a happy compromise.

FASTER RAY TRACING—RAY RECURSION LIMIT

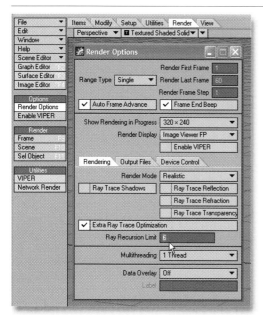

Have you ever noticed that when you turn on say, reflections, LightWave rendering slows down? Well, there's a little value setting you can change that can help this annoying problem. Go to Render Options, under the Render tab. There's a default value setting of 16 in a requester labeled Ray Recursion Limit. Set this baby to about 2 or 4, and watch your renders fly! Well, okay, they won't fly, but they do render faster with ray tracing turned on. One note, however: If you have transparencies active for certain surfaces, you might encounter some rendering errors. If so, just increase the value a bit.

    LIMITED REGION, LIMITED RENDER

So you got this really big scene cooking, right? But there's one nasty little area within the render that is just gettin' up yer crawl. With each change to the area, be it a surface or lighting change, you need to render again to see change. And, with such a big scene, big renders follow. So here's a little feature that can help you isolate just that one area for rendering. Go to the Camera panel and select Limited Region toward the top left of the panel. You can choose with or without borders. Then, back in Layout, go to the Camera view, press the "L" key, and click and drag from one of the upper corners of the screen. When you press the "L" key, a soft yellow outline appears. Drag this outline from the different edges to change the size of the region, and then you can click and drag it from the center to move it into a desired location. Then, when you press F9 for a render test, only that region will render.

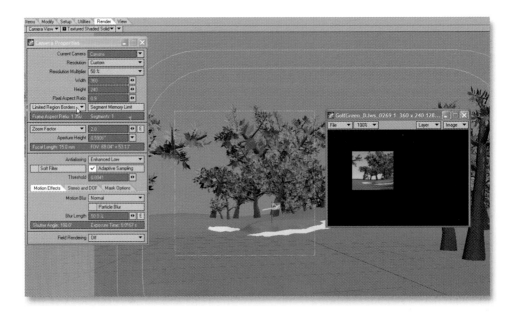

But wait! There's more! You can render full animations like this! Set up a limited region render the same way, but instead of an F9 test render, just render the animation as you normally would. To get back to a regular full-screen render, just go back to the Camera panel and turn off Limited Region.

   RPF EXPORT INTO AFTER EFFECTS

Sometimes you can't do everything in LightWave. Yeah, it's sad but true. But when you need to use a third-party application to composite or create a different type effect, you might be using Adobe After Effects. LightWave now talks with third-party programs better than before. What you can do is save not just your render, but also the data included with the render, such as the camera motion. Render out an image sequence with the Extended RPF Image Filter found under the Image Processing tab, from the Window drop-down list in Layout. Then load the sequence into After Effects 5.5 Production Bundle. Make a simple composition from the imported sequence, and then right-click on the RPF layer. Select Keyframe Assistant

and then RPF Camera Import. What you'll be greeted with is an animated camera that moves just like your LightWave camera. Use this for added enhancements to your render!

   RLA EXPORT

Sometimes when you use compositing programs such as Eyeon's Digital Fusion, Bauhaus Software's Mirage, or Adobe's After Effects, you need more than a simple RGB image. 3D rendered images out of LightWave can contain a lot of information. To maximize the data within these images, you can use the RLA saver from the Image Filters, found under the Image Processing tab within the Window drop-down list in Layout, when rendering out an animation. The RLA saver gives you the option of saving the depth of an image, the UV buffer, the material buffer, and more. Compositing programs can use this data, which gives you ultimate flexibility for things like layering, compositing, and keying.

RENDERING IN LAYERS

Perhaps saving image sequences with embedded data using the RPF or RLA savers just doesn't cut your mustard. Maybe that damn technical director breathing down your neck keeps telling you that the compositor needs the character pass, while the other guy needs the backgrounds pass, and so on. Basically, if you want ultimate control of your 3D renders, you should render in multiple passes. Render out a pass with just the set your character walks on. Then render out a pass with just the character. The only difference in these two renders is that one shows the background and one shows just the character. Cameras, lights, and motions all remain the same. By having multiple passes (as many as you like), you have complete control over shadows, density, depth, and more when using these passes in a compositing program. Try it! How? It's easy. From the Scene Editor, turn off the items you don't want to render. Or, you can tell certain objects to be Unseen By Camera by checking that option in the Object Properties panel.

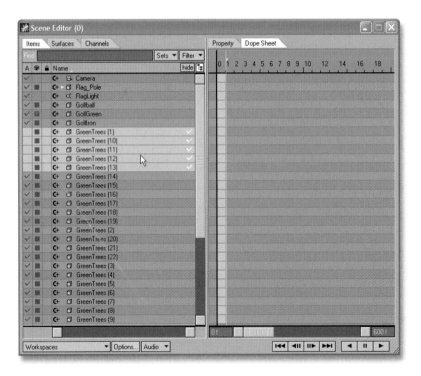

CREATE A RACK FOCUS SHOT

Rack Focus? No, this is not something out of a men's magazine, but rather a movie and television technique that forces the viewers' eye to a specific action or position in the frame. In LightWave, you can use the Digital Confusion plug-in to create an animated depth of field shot. Using a simple null object in Layout, position the null at a particular frame you want in focus. Then move the null around to keep that particular area in focus. You can move the null from one character to another as the characters have a discussion to change the camera's focus. Go to the Window drop-down list in Layout and select Image Processing. Find the Digital Confusion plug-in under the Add Image Filter plug-in list. In the Digital Confusion plug-in panel (double-click it to open it), you can tell the tool to use the null object as the AutoFocus object. Make it like a real movie!

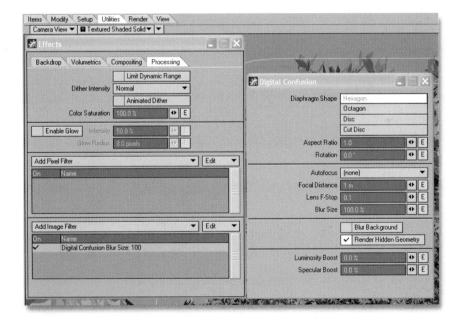

   WHO NEEDS A GPS MAP WHEN YOU HAVE A CAMERA MAP?

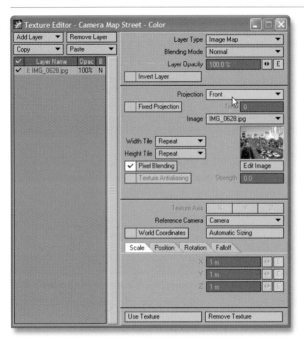

Photoreal imaging is totally cool, dude! Forget the messy radiosity renders and sticky complex models. Just use photographs! Let's say that you have a digital camera, and you've taken photos of a building on a city street. Using LightWave's camera mapping techniques, you can turn those photos into 3D objects. Start by loading a photo into Modeler's background. Make basic box geometry to represent the building within the photograph, and make other simple geometry for roads and cars, and so on. Load those into Layout. Then put the photograph into the background of

Layout (Compositing tab) and open the Surface Editor. Use a Front type projection of the same image onto the objects. Now all you need to do is line up your camera and the objects so their edges match the lines in the photograph. Balance any lighting and move your camera around the scene. It's instant 3D realism without the headache.

SAVE AN ALPHA PASS

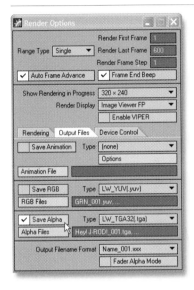

That pesky technical director is back and bugging you to render "just an alpha pass" of your current project. How do you do that? An *alpha pass* is just a black-and-white pass of your 3D animation, sort of like a cookie cutter, if you will. Well, if you open the Render Options panel from the Render tab, down toward the bottom under Output Files is an option named Save Alpha. Select this, choose the file type you want, and when you render your animation, a black-and-white mask of your animation is saved as well. You can use this in compositing for exact keying. Additionally, if you render out say, a QuickTime movie or AVI file, choose a particular codec that has an option for saving an alpha channel. And, if you save just 32-bit RGB images, your full-color renders will contain an embedded alpha channel. Ah, choices!

   ## 64 BIT! AND WE'RE NOT TALKING COMMODORE!

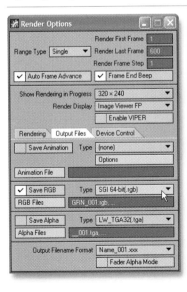

64 bit is a hot topic, and this is a completely different thing from a Commodore 64. What's that? It's not important right now. What is important is that LightWave supports the rendering of 64-bit images. Why is this good? It's because 64-bit imaging reduces color banding, has more accurate pixel resolution, and makes compositing that much better. To render 64 bit, go to the Render Options panel under the Render tab and choose the SGI 64-bit image saver from the Save RGB option. Conversely, you can save 48-bit images!

   RENDERING FOR PRINT

Don't you just hate it when that crazy print guy calls you up and yells at you that your rendered image is "only 72 dpi"? See, LightWave is made for video and film, so the resolution is set up that way. Often, those "clever" print people don't know anything about video and don't realize that your rendered pixels are just fine for print. All they need to do is change the DPI setting in their imaging program (such as Adobe Photoshop) but turn off resample. Now, how do you calculate a render for printout of LightWave? It's so easy that you'll wonder why you didn't use this feature sooner. Let's say that your publisher says it needs an 8×10 image at 300 dpi. In LightWave, go to the Utilities tab. Click the Additional drop-down

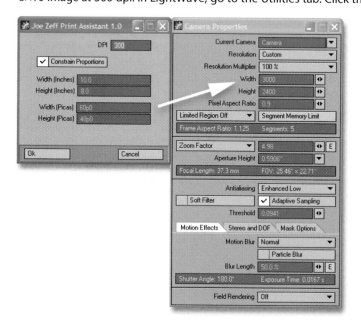

list, and select the Print Assistant plug-in. Here, set the DPI to 300, turn off Constrain if needed, and type in the appropriate width and height you need, such as 8×10. (You can actually use any of the fields to solve the calculations.) Click OK and open the Camera panel. Your pixel resolution is now adjusted for you. Simply render and send off to that smart layout guy.

SINGLE SEGMENT RENDERS

If you've just installed LightWave and figured out how to render a frame—or even better, an animation—good for you! Now, you might have noticed that the render sort of did the top half of the frame first and then the bottom. What's up with that? Well, by default, LightWave sets a low segment memory. This tells LightWave how much memory to use for rendering. In the Camera panel, however, you can change this. Open the panel, and set this baby up past 20. Don't worry: This doesn't mean to use 20MB of memory for rendering every frame. What this tells LightWave is that if you need to, you can use up to but no more than 20MB of memory when rendering. If you have a lot of RAM, set this to 60 or so and leave it alone. Make it the default value when it asks you. Now when you render at video resolution, the renders will be pumped out in one segment. If you increase the resolution to a print resolution size, rendering in segments might return. If so, increase this value until it's back to one segment again. The benefit of doing this is for speed and for certain plug-ins that like a single segment.

    LOW ON MEMORY?

Maybe you're the type of person who skimped on memory when you got your computer system. You shouldn't do this, of course, but we're not here to lecture you. If you're low on memory and having trouble rendering, just go to the Camera panel and decrease the Segment Memory Limit. This slows down your renders a little bit, but it takes RAM away from your rendering, saving system resources. Hey, slower renders are better than no renders!

   ## AVI OR MOV OR RGB?

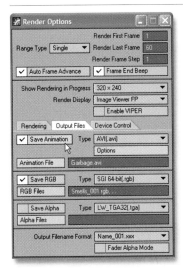

Have you ever wondered just how to decipher all the different types of render options? Really, who needs all this? How are AVI, MOV, RGB, and the others different? How do you choose? Our tip to you is this: Render in the highest quality possible, without compression. Use AVI or MOV files for most previews. Often, rendering to an AVID system, for example, or perhaps a KONA card or VT3, requires QuickTime MOV or AVI files. If so, you'll need to install a special codec that's usually supplied by the particular video card manufacturer. That's fine. But in ordinary cases when you're rendering for a multiple pass, or perhaps bringing the animation back into LightWave for further work, it's often a good idea to render out RGB sequences. Not to mention if the power fails with one frame left, and you lose the entire AVI or MOV file because it is incomplete! (D'oh!) And no, don't use JPG sequences. Use good-quality sequences without compression, such as TIF, TGA, or PNG files. Remember: Garbage in, garbage out! But hey, you can always render both images and animation at the same time, too!

   ## ARBITRARY RENDERS? GET IT TOGETHER!

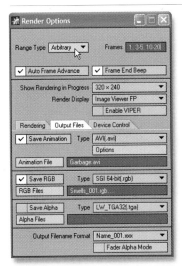

These days, high tech prevails. Of course, that has nothing to do with this tip. Have you ever wanted to render just a few certain frames? And what if those frames take 10 minutes each? Guess what? You're not a babysitter—you're an animator! You used to have to render the first frame and then wait. Then you would change frames, render, and so on. Well, be gone, old ways! Now you can go to the Render Options panel under the Render tab (if you have any amount of sense, you should already know where this panel is by now) and select Arbitrary for Range Type. Then enter in the desired frames you want to render, and go get some sleep!

  RENDER WITH INFO

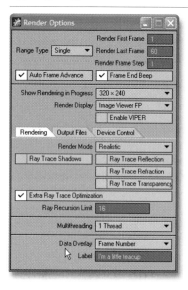

Perhaps you're one of the lucky ones to be working on a LightWave animation to be used for television or film. Often, this type of work requires many changes and variations. Argh! The madness! How do you keep track? Well, aside from learning how to take notes and be organized, you can also add data to your renders. Go to the Render Options panel. At the bottom of the Rendering tab, click on Data Overlay and choose a feature, such as Frame Number. In the requester, enter some necessary data like **test 1**, a client name, or even a copyright. When you play back the animation, you'll have a visual reference of what you're looking at.

PROTECT YOUR RENDERS

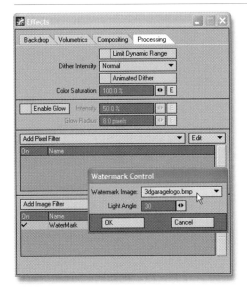

All right, you've figured out how to use the program. You've convinced a willing person to actually pay you. But before that person pays you, he wants to "see" how his job will look. Often, this is a ploy to see the work without actually paying for it. People like to do this, and to protect yourself and your work, you should add a watermark to the render. A *watermark* is a simple image file you can place on the rendered frames that looks embossed. Television stations do it all the time when you're watching their channel. You can do it by selecting the Watermark plug-in from the Image Filter drop-down list in the Image Processing tab. Get there from the Window drop-down list in Layout. Open it, and choose the image you want to use as a watermark, such as your name or logo with a copyright. Be sure to create a black image the size of your render. Make a white logo or copyright somewhere on the frame where you want it to appear in the render. A typical place is in the bottom-right corner. Then save the black-and-white image and apply it as a watermark. LightWave then embosses the white part of the image over your render. Oh, you'll need to load the image through LightWave's Image Editor first if you didn't figure that out.

   STORYBOARD RENDERS

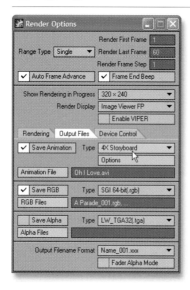

Silly clients. Storyboards are created before you do your animations! Well, not all the time. Every once in a while when you are creating an animation for a client, he wants to see your progress. Typically, animators render out various single frames to highlight the action. But did you know that you can set one option and render your entire animation as a storyboard? Sure thing. Go to the Render Options panel; under the Output Files tab, under the Animation Type drop-down list, you can select either 4x Storyboard, or just Storyboard as an animation saver. The 4x Storyboard saver saves a rendered image 4 panels tall and 4 panels wide. Cool! More time to sleep!

   BLACK-AND-WHITE RENDERS

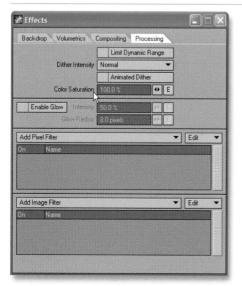

It's not often done, but it's a really cool effect. Perhaps because 3D is so colorful and cool, we're all just used to it like that. But did you know that you can take the color out of your render without extra processing? You can even animate the color saturation over time. Just go to the Image Processing tab from the Window drop-down list in Layout. Color Saturation defaults to 100%, full color. Bring this to 0%, and your render will be black and white. Click the E button and set an envelope to animate the color saturation.

LOADING A SEQUENCE INTO…LIGHTWAVE? WHAT??

So the client needed a sequence of frames for their animation. They show up to see the work, but you don't have it compiled into a format you can play for them. You could load the sequence into Premiere, VT3, or Final Cut, but what if all you have is LightWave? This trick will save the day. Load the sequence of images into the background of an empty scene and render the scene to an animation format like AVI, MOV, and so on. There is no geometry in the scene, so it will render very fast. Just make sure that the camera's resolution matches the resolution of your images.

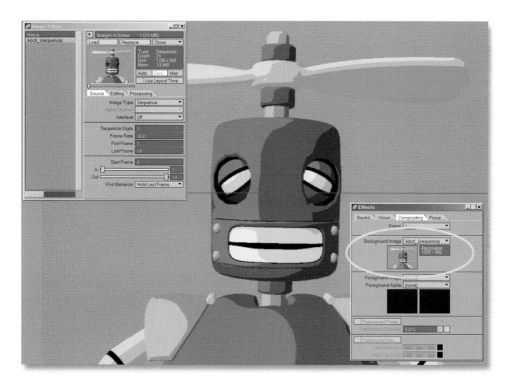

Tricky Dick

Who said size doesn't matter? Sure, it does—at least when it comes to tips!

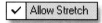

Tricky Dick
Presidential Size Tips

The length of a helpful tip, when it is typed up for the reader to digest—might be pretty short. The time saved, however, even by the shortest of tips, can be huge. If a single tip can save you 5 minutes a day, that's 25 minutes for a regular work week—or 1,300 minutes per work year. That's right, 21 2/3 hours. That's nearly a full day saved. Or how about almost four work days? Suddenly that little four-line tip does seem a bit bigger, doesn't it? Makes it look downright…presidential!

  ANIMATED ROPES

Did you know that it's pretty easy to animate ropes or tentacles in LightWave without a bunch of messy third-party plug-ins? Yeah! It's called Spline Control. First, select your object you want to move, then under the Deform tab in the Object properties panel, select the Add Displacement plug-in list. Choose Spline Control. Double-click the plug-in to open it after it's been selected, and choose how many control points you want, perhaps 8. Go back to Layout and click the SplineControl button you've added, and you'll see a spline in your object. Grab and pull and animate away.

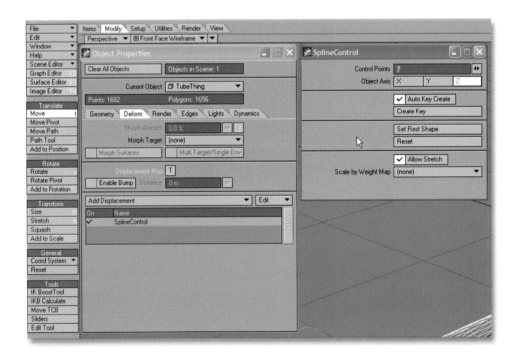

QUICK AGING

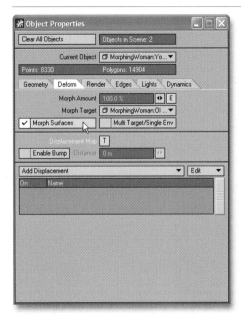

Years ago, way back in the Stone Age when LightWave was on the Amiga computer, there was a feature that needed to be used to accomplish some everyday tasks. That feature is now long forgotten but still useful. Have you ever wanted to make a surface age? You know, have a wooden chair turn from new to old, or a young woman change into an old lady? How? It's so easy! Bring your model into LightWave Modeler. Make sure that this object has a surface name such as "surface one," copy this object, and paste it down in a new layer. Give the copy a new name, and make any adjustments to it, such as adding bags to the eyes if it's an old woman. Be sure to name each layer, or at least remember which model is which! Save out the object. In Layout, load the object. LightWave remembers that the single object has layers, so you only need to load the single object. Select Layer 2, and press the "p" key to open the Object Properties panel. In the Deform tab, select Layer 2 of your object as the Morph Target, making sure that the Current Object is Layer 1. Then click the Morph Surfaces check box, also in the Deform tab. Next, click the E button to open the Graph Editor for Morph Target, and create a keyframe at frame 60 with a value of 100%. Close the Graph Editor and then click the Render tab of the Object Properties panel. The last setting you need is to make Layer 2 invisible. Drag Object Dissolve to 100% for Layer 2. With any necessary surfacing and lighting in place, render your scene and watch your object change!

     USE LAYOUT AS A MODELER!

Yes, you, too, can use your LightWave Layout as a Modeler. Why fuss with those messy Modeler panels and tools? Perhaps you need to create a cool-looking asteroid. A simple chunky ball loaded into Layout can be turned into a rough rock with a displacement map. After you've applied, say, a procedural texture to crunch up the space rock, use the Save Trans (Transformed) Object command from the File drop-down menu to save the adjusted object. This also works with an object that has dynamics, such as Cloth_FX. A great example would be draping a tablecloth over a table. Let the computer do the work! The next time you load the object, it will be deformed as if the displacement map is still applied, which is useful for saving render times. Your object is already displaced; therefore, LightWave needs to calculate less. On a single object, this doesn't save you diddly do, but add that to a huge scene with hundreds of objects, and every little bit of time saving helps.

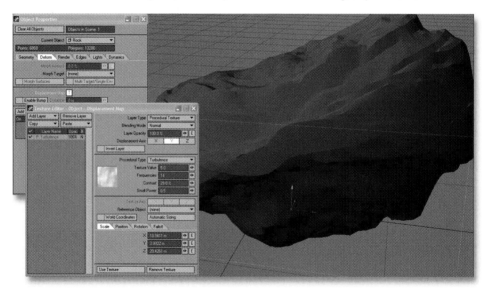

MULTIPLE BACKGROUND IMAGES

Placing a loaded image in LightWave Layout's backdrop via the Compositing tab (Ctrl+F7) allows you to composite, but it also simplifies renders with multiple passes. You can render out a portion of an animation, such as the moving background, reload it into LightWave, and put it in the backdrop. From there, you can animate just your desired objects over the backdrop. That background image does not react to lighting, and you can't you cast shadows on it. This is great for those annoying directors who require multiple render passes. But what if you wanted that backdrop change to a different backdrop? Or you use multiple backdrops? LightWave only allows one image to be put into the backdrop. Or does it? Head on into the Image Editor. Select the primary image or movie you're using in your background. Click the Processing tab within the Image Editor, and load the Textured Filter from the Add Filter drop-down. Double-click the Textured Filter after it's loaded, and then click the Texture button that appears. LightWave's Texture Editor pops up, and in that panel, you can specify another image to layer on top of the original. Set the Layer Opacity envelope to animate this image to fade up or down over time. In addition, you can play with the various blending modes for added effects. Need another image? Just add a new Image Map layer and do it again!

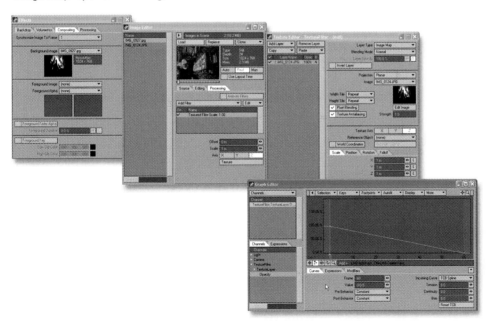

    THE LIGHTWAVE IMAGE MANIPULATOR

Perhaps you can't afford Adobe After Effects, or you haven't yet picked up Eyeon's Digital Fusion. No worries, mate! You have more control over your rendered animations and video clips than you might think. Yes, we said video clips! Say that you took some video of your dog Skip pooping on the neighbor's lawn. It's just what you need to complete that never-ending home video, but you need to stylize it a bit, perhaps add a night vision look, or blur it or something. So here's what you do. Load the clip, be it a QuickTime or AVI file, into LightWave. Do this from the Image Editor (Ctrl+F4). Then click the Compositing tab (Ctrl+F7) and set the loaded clip (or single image) as the background image. Next, click the Processing tab in the Image Editor, and from the Add Filter drop-down list, pick a filter of choice, such as NightVision. Press F9 to render, and LightWave applies your chosen filter. Set up the render the way you like, and you're on your way to having processed video. Note that you can double-click the chosen plug-in filter to set any parameters that it might have.

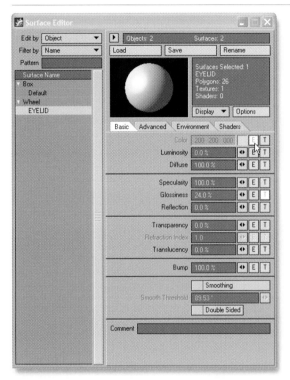

CLICKED THAT E BUTTON, DID YA?

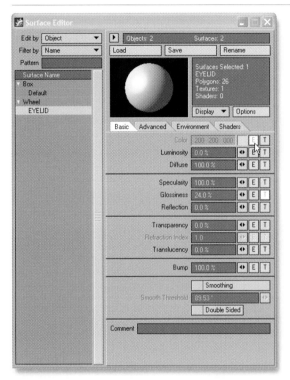

All right, really quick tip here. Well, it's not so much a tip as a piece of information. It happens to everyone. You're working away, clicking along minding your own business and all of a sudden, you're in the Graph Editor. What the hell? You close the Graph Editor, but still, that damn E button remains pressed, not allowing you to change the numeric value. You press Ctrl+z to undo, and nothing happens! Argh! Then it happens with the T button! What will you do? Okay, this is tough. Are you ready? Hold the Shift key, and then click the E. All fixed. You'll get my bill in the mail.

  CLOTH STRETCH FIX

When working with ClothFX in Layout, LightWave's cloth generation system, you sometimes get a weird stretching of the material. Most people go in and change the stretch limit to try and adjust, and that works for the most part, except for right at the front of the simulation. Even though the stretch limit is set, after a flag, let's say, gets into motion, it sort of stretches out quickly and then recedes to its determined stretch. To fix this, simply set your Layout animation first frame to a negative number, such as –60. This will give a 2-second preroll to the simulation. Set this and calculate the simulation. Make sure you save your simulation. When you're finished, set the first frame in the timeline back to frame 0, and your object will no longer jump when it begins moving. It will be in perfect motion at the start of your animation.

INFINITE PARTICLES

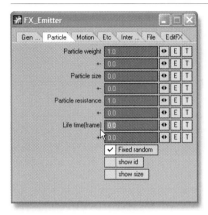

LightWave 8's new particle system is pretty cool, and it's easy to use, too. But one of the first things everyone does is set the Life Time in the Particle tab to a higher value, such as 300, rather than the default 60. It's at that point people then realize that 300 is not enough, so they go back and set it higher. Ugh! What a pain! Instead, set this value to 0, and your particles will live forever. Peace be with you.

RIDE THE WAVE—WITH A FILTER

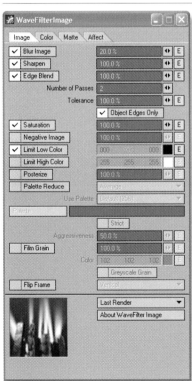

Way back when, there was a really nifty plug-in for LightWave called WaveFilter. Mike Reed created this, and along the way, it sort of got misplaced. NewTek found it, and it's updated for LightWave 8. We think that's just swell, and you should, too. Load up your favorite scene, or even just put an image in the background of Layout. Head on over to the Image Processing tab (Ctrl+F8), and from the Add Image Filter drop-down list, select the WaveFilter plug-in. Double-click to open the options, and in this panel, you can set up cool post-processing features for your renders! You can adjust saturation, blurs, or even sharpen. You can posterize your render, and more. There's a nifty little preview as well. Check it out!

  BE IN CONTROL OF YOUR SELECTIONS

When you're selecting in the Perspective view in LightWave Modeler, you tend to get a bit ahead of yourself. We know, it's okay; everyone does it. So, it is best to press and hold the Shift key and select using a click of the mouse per selection. Using the Lasso selection (right mouse button), or drag-selecting, tends to select polygons that might not even be visible in the Perspective view. The click-select technique usually does a much better job of selecting exactly what you want.

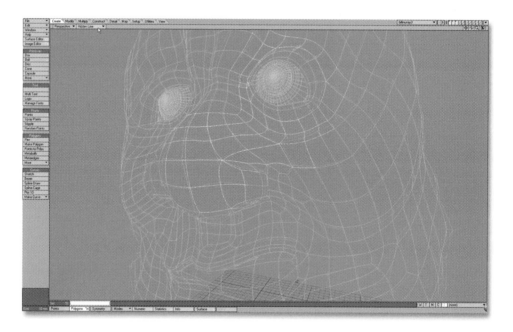

     ## STILL CAN'T GET THOSE POLYGONS SELECTED? TRY THIS...

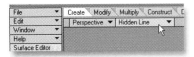

If you've read the previous tip, and you're still having trouble selecting points or polygons in Modeler's Perspective view, you need to use this cool new mode. At the top of your viewport, you can set the view style. Change it to Hidden Line. This handy little mode only shows you the geometry that's facing you. By the same token, you'll only select the points or polygons that you can see. Brilliant, ain't it?

     ## BAKING SURFACES JUST NOT COOKING FOR YOU?

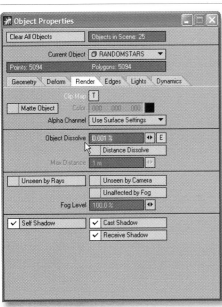

If you've discovered LightWave's powerful Surface Baking techniques, you might have found yourself a new friend. This handy feature bakes, or freezes, the surface of choice, elevating heavy-duty calculations at render time. Sometimes, though, your surfaces just won't bake. This is because LightWave culls the geometry it does not see. So, all you have to do is set the Object Dissolve to .001%, and everything will bake accordingly.

   ## STAND-IN OBJECTS FOR BETTER SYSTEM RESPONSE

Yeah, we know. You have the latest and greatest computer on the block. Sorry? What? You don't? Oh, good. We have another tip for you that can help with the huge-ass complex scenes. Have you ever noticed that the more you add to a LightWave scene, the slower your system becomes? Until we figure that one out, what you can do is make a stand-in object! That's right—you can make your own 3D stunt double. Go into Modeler and load the complex model of choice. Then save it to a safe place. In a new layer, draw a box; perhaps subpatch slightly to represent the object you just saved. Make this a low polygon model that merely represents the basic shape of your main object. Save this as a new object. Use this object to set up your animations and move around Layout quickly. If it is critical that you have the actual subpatched object in your scene, then set the display subpatch level to 0 (zero). When it's time to render, select Replace Object in Layout and replace this stand-in with the real thing. Work smarter, not harder!

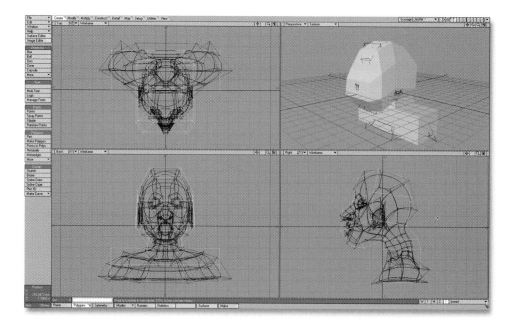

ENTERING AND EXITING VALUES

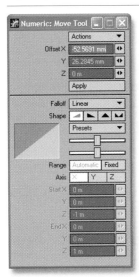

This might not seem like much of a tip, but if you've ever been bitten by this, you'll appreciate it. Let's say that you're entering some numeric values in Modeler. You think you have it all together and press the "t" key to move the object. Suddenly, your object freaks out! Basically, you never exited your numeric fields, so the "t" you typed was put into a value! To avoid this in the future, as soon as you're done entering a value, press the Esc key to exit the panel. By the same token, have you ever entered a value and not had it take effect? This is because you must press the Enter key on your keyboard to—get this—enter the data!

   ## ASSEMBLING LOAD FROM SCENE

When you're working in Layout, there is an option under the Items tab under the Load heading called From Scene. Is this a typo? Not really. It's a cool feature that allows you to load one scene into your current scene. For example, let's say that you're creating the next great masterpiece that will gross $300 million at the box office. Your main scene is composed of a two-mile stretch of road, houses, cars, planes, goofy trees, and any other strange object you've made. Now, you need to make the main character walk down the street, but first you need to set up his textures and character rig. Doing this within this huge scene is not only a possible danger to your existing scene, but your system also will not respond as well with so much going on. So, save your main scene, and in a new empty scene, set up your character. Save this as its own scene. Load the main scene again, and then use Load From Scene to load the character scene into this one. This is really useful for setups that require multiple hierarchies of parenting, or special lighting rigs, and more.

ANONYMOUS RENDERS—HIDE FROM CAMERA

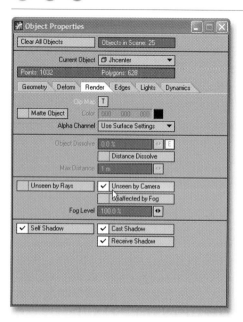

It's fun to trick your viewer. In the real video and film world, you pretty much get what you see through the camera. But in the computer world, you get what you want to see. Let's say that you need to create a scene full of reflective balls. In one of the balls, you need a 3D car to drive by. So, you add a car, drive it by, and the car shows up in the reflection. But wait! You don't actually want this in your scene; you only want the reflection. That's easy enough! Select the object, press the "P" key for Object Properties, and under the Render tab, select Unseen by Camera. Now, the camera that is rendering the animation will ignore the car, but nothing else will!

   FIXING BAKED UV MAPS

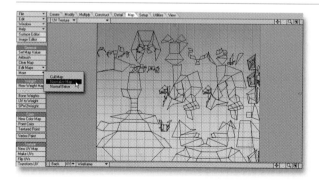

Baking in LightWave is cool and useful, especially for things like radiosity. But often when you bake an image, all the polygons within a UV map are down at the bottom right of the image. To fix this, you can use the Normalize Map tool, which stretches the UV Map perfectly into the UV space. You do this in Modeler when you create the UV Map. And, you can use this for any other UV Map as well, not just when baking.

COLLISION STUNT DOUBLE

To save time on dynamic calculations, use a stand-in that won't take as long to calculate. Default Collision objects work great for times when per-polygon collision isn't needed. At the end of the day, as long as the animation looks right, how you got there doesn't matter. Sometimes being a cheater is a good thing.

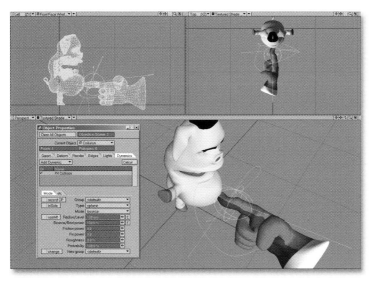

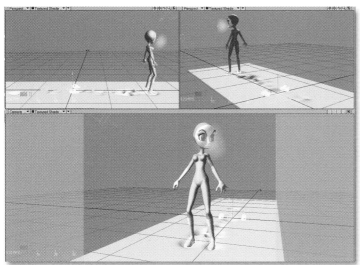

  HATE TO TYPE?

You and me both. Nothing is worse then typing in a long expression only to find that you left one letter out of a 26-letter channel name. There is a solution for those of us who can't spell or type, so don't worry. All you have to do is right-click on the channel name and choose Append to Expression. This operation will place the channel name in the Value field. What a time-saver!

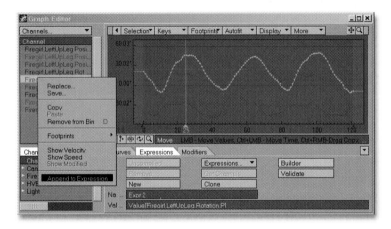

   SHAPE UP OR SHIP OUT

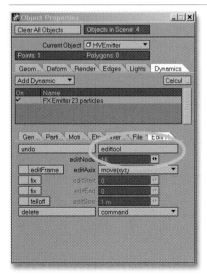

Ever had a point shoot out away from the cluster, and no matter what settings you used, you couldn't fix it? Never fear—Edit tool is here. The Edit tool in the EditFX tab will give you the ability to edit each individual point. For some situations, you can even use the Delete button on the EditFX tab to remove the point or points that are giving you trouble.

GOTTA BONE TO PICK

Have a bone or object that is in a hard-to-reach area? Proxy Pick along with custom objects could be the solution for you. Proxy Pick translates the selection of one object, known as the proxy, into the selection of another, known as the target. This is useful for choosing small but crucial items out of complex, crowded scenes. Note: You will need to disable this tool when you want to select the proxy rather than the target.

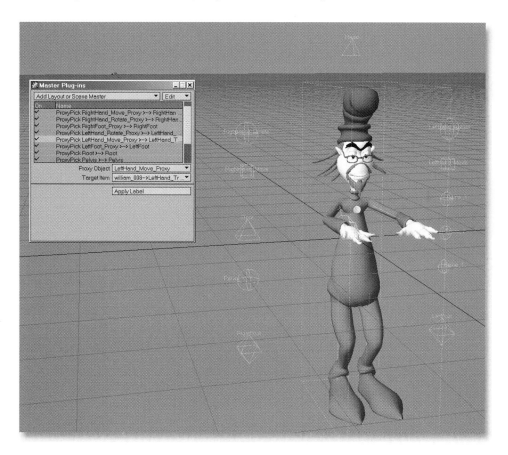

  CLEAN IT UP

Proxy Items cluttering up your already cluttered scene? Give the Item Picker a go. Item Picker displays the Quick Pick panel. You can instantly select frequently used items in your scene just by clicking on the item's name in the list. The more complex your scene, the more indispensable Item Picker becomes.

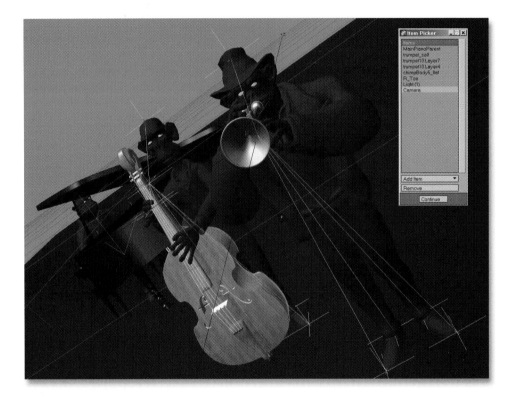

INDEX

informIT

www.informit.com

YOUR GUIDE TO IT REFERENCE

New Riders has partnered with **InformIT.com** to bring technical information to your desktop. Drawing from New Riders authors and reviewers to provide additional information on topics of interest to you, **InformIT.com** provides free, in-depth information you won't find anywhere else.

Articles

Keep your edge with thousands of free articles, in-depth features, interviews, and IT reference recommendations— all written by experts you know and trust.

Online Books

Answers in an instant from **InformIT Online Books'** 600+ fully searchable online books.

POWERED BY
Safari

Catalog

Review online sample chapters, author biographies, and customer rankings, and choose exactly the right book from a selection of more than 5,000 titles.

New Riders

www.newriders.com

Maximize Your Impact

As THE game resource, NRG books explore programming, design, art, and celebrity savvy. NRG takes you behind the scenes... revealing insider secrets like never before.

1592730094
George "Fat Man" Sanger
US$35.00

1592730078
David Freeman
Foreword by Will Wright
US$49.99

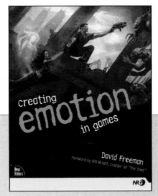

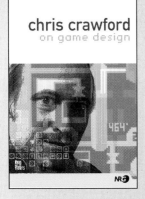

0131460994
Chris Crawford
US$39.99

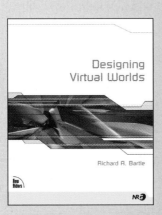

0131018167
Richard A. Bartle
US$49.99

0735713073
Marc Mencher
US$29.99

New Riders

0735713677
Marc Saltzman
US$49.99

0735713634
Andrew Rollings,
Dave Morris
US$49.99

1592730000
Jessica Mulligan,
Bridgette Patrovsky
US$49.99

1592730051
David Brackeen
US$49.99

0131020099
Daniel Sánchez-Crespo Dalmau
US$49.99

1592730019
Andrew Rollings,
Ernest Adams
US$49.99

Maya 5 Killer Tips
Eric Hanson
0735713731
US$39.99

Inside LightWave 8
Dan Ablan
0735713685
US$59.99
July 2004

[digital] Texturing & Painting
Owen Demers
0735709181
US$55.00

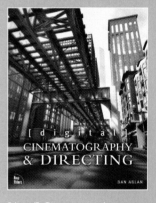

[digital] Cinematography
& Directing
Dan Ablan
0735712581
US$45.00

3ds max 6 Killer Tips
Jon A. Bell
0735713863
US$39.99

[digital] Lighting & Rendering
Jeremy Birn
1562059548
US$50.00

VOICES
THAT MATTER™

New
Riders

WWW.NEWRIDERS.COM